THE TEN WORST FRAUDS AGAINST AMERICA'S SENIORS

By Jed J. Richardson

Introduction by Mary Martin
Chairman of the Board of Directors
and Executive Director
of The Seniors Coalition

THE SENIORS COALITION

"The Ten Worst Frauds
Against America's Seniors"

First Edition

Library of Congress Catalog Card Number: 98-86013

ISBN 0-9648635-2-9

Cover art by Graphic Expressions
Book design by The Design Studio

Published by The Seniors Coalition, Inc.
11166 Main Street, Suite 302
Fairfax, Virginia 22030
(703) 591-0663

Published in the United States of America

THE TEN WORST FRAUDS AGAINST AMERICA'S SENIORS

Jed J. Richardson

TABLE OF CONTENTS

Acknowledgment

Grateful acknowledgment is made to the
members, supporters, and staff of
The Seniors Coalition
who made this book possible.

INTRODUCTION

By Mary M. Martin, Chairman

THE SENIORS COALITION

Americans joke knowingly about two famous lies: "The check is in the mail," and "I'm from the government, and I'm here to help."

All of us have heard them, and while we may chuckle at these phrases, they do highlight the fact that what we sometimes hear from our government officials is not necessarily true. In fact, more often than not, the statements we read in our newspapers and hear on television from our leaders are simply false.

More disturbing, much of what we hear is part of a larger scheme to mislead and outright deceive the American people about the political realities of issues important to us.

This book provides an invaluable service to American seniors by shedding light on a number of critical public policy issues affecting the quality of life for all of us.

As a retired senior citizen, I believe strongly that our leaders owe us better. I make decisions every day about how I am going to handle my personal finances, and many of those decisions are directly impacted by public policies about which our leaders are simply not being truthful.

The Ten Worst Frauds Against America's Seniors focuses on ten important issues that every senior should know about. These are issues that impact our lives, and, without some action, threaten to erode our financial well-being, our ability to access health care services when we need them, and a host of other issues that, if mishandled, will diminish the overall quality of life we have a right to expect in retirement.

Hopefully, this book will be a catalyst for action in Washington and in State Legislatures across America. It is clear to me that too many politicians give only lip service to senior issues, and frankly, most of these politicians take senior voters for granted.

As pointed out powerfully in this book, seniors should not be pigeon-holed politically as being interested only in Social Security and Medicare. Those issues are important, but they represent just a few of the public policy debates about which we care deeply.

I have also seen enough double-talk among our elected officials to have eroded my confidence that our political system will inspire integrity and fairness. We simply have to keep our politicians' feet to the fire every day to ensure that we protect the future we've earned. Washington is a town where compromises are routine, and too often they are compromises of principle rather than of issues.

As Chairman of The Seniors Coalition, I see first hand what these frauds do to honest, hard-working seniors in America. Jed Richardson has captured an important agenda for change. If effected, these changes would alleviate many disadvantages we seniors face every day. Most importantly, these changes would put government in a position always intended: helping rather than hindering. And that's no joke.

FRAUD: a) deceit, trickery; *specif:* intentional perversion of truth in order to induce another to part with something of value or to surrender a legal right; b) an act of deceiving or misrepresenting: TRICK 2 a: a person who is not who he or she pretends to be: IMPOSTER: *also:* one who defrauds: CHEAT b: one that is not what it seems or is represented to be.

Merriam Webster's Collegiate Dictionary
Tenth Edition 1994

When a person thinks of fraud, it sometimes is viewed in a very narrow legal context. But outside of the strictures of the law, we are subjected to frauds every day where something is represented to be one thing, and when all the facts are known we find out it is quite different. In the world of politics, there is an enormous amount of deception and trickery going on as politicians and bureaucrats try to develop some favorable spin on what they have done, are about to do, or hope to do in the future. For the average American, that generally means it is going to cost them some money. This book attempts to shed light on the political frauds that are rampant in America in the hope that educated seniors can take appropriate steps to protect themselves.

FRAUD #1:

A NATIONAL HEALTH CARE SYSTEM IS NEEDED FOR AMERICA

In his book *The Dog That Bites,* James Thurber writes how his mother often apologized for the misbehavior of Muggs, the family dog, by claiming that the dog was not well. "He may not have been well," Thurber observes, "but he was indeed terribly strong." So it is for the health care plan envisioned by Bill and Hillary Clinton for all Americans. It may not be well, but it is indeed terribly strong.

Bill and Hillary Clinton made national health care reform the centerpiece of their Presidency as they labored in 1992 and 1993 to convince the Congress and America that the American health care delivery system was in desperate need of a major restructuring.

To be sure, the Congress has its own spotty record of tinkering with the health care delivery system in ways that create far more problems than they solve. You can just look at the Congress' 1989 approval of the so-called Medicare Catastrophic Coverage Act which dramatically increased monthly premiums for Medicare beneficiaries and forced seniors into paying for something they did not want.

Led by The Seniors Coalition, concerned seniors delivered a powerful message to the Congress that they would not tolerate such huge increases in Medicare premiums. Indeed, for many, these premium increases forced the horrible choice between being able to afford Medicare premiums or paying for food or monthly rent. It was a message that Congress could not ignore, and this ill-fated bill was repealed some nine months after its initial passage. That experience should have been a political message for anyone who thought they could burden consumers with unjustifiably higher costs just to expand the health care bureaucracy.

For the Clintons, Bill and Hillary brought to Washington a recast liberal program that has been rejected many times in the past. While they would like to hide behind sneaky new titles and deceptive rhetoric, the Clinton health care reform plan is one thing, and one thing only: socialized medicine. And the Clintons plan to keep pecking away at our current freedoms even though they lost the battle to enact their sweeping program of socialized medicine.

Here's what the Clinton socialized medicine plan tries to do:

♦ **Eliminate choice of doctor by seniors.** Under the Clinton plan, all seniors would be forced into Medicare HMOs. Some HMOs do provide quality service, but seniors should have a choice. Most important, for those HMOs who provide good service, you can bet it is because of the competition for patients. If you take away the competition, you can say goodbye to quality. Seniors can forget choosing their own doctor or buying their own private insurance under the Clinton plan.

♦ **Allow a gross invasion of privacy by the government on every American.** Under the Clinton plan, every American would be required to carry an identification card that would be the key for government to collect data. That means thousands of bureaucrats in Washington would have total access to health history and financial data on every American.

♦ **Make criminals of health care providers.** The only way the Clinton plan can work is to force everyone, including doctors, to participate. There would be criminal penalties for any health care providers who offer private pay services for covered benefits or who offer services outside of the limited benefit package for those who choose to pay for those services themselves.

Even the Clintons' supporters agree that the failed Clinton health care plan was largely the victim of its own crushing breadth of coverage, the huge costs that would cripple the budget, and far-reaching new entitlement programs that would have created huge new bureaucracies and the total destruction of consumer choice. The "cradle-to-grave" concept of health care coverage is not in the best interest of any American citizen, but that is precisely what the Clinton crusade for socializing our heath care system is dedicated to delivering.

When the U.S. Congress rendered its judgment on the Clinton health care reform plan in 1994, many thought that was the end of it. But that was pollyannaish thinking at best. Bill and Hillary Clinton, with their dedicated band of big-government bullies, have hunkered in to enact the Clinton plan piecemeal.

"If what I tried before won't work, maybe we can do it another way," Clinton mused in a speech in the fall of 1997. "That's what we have tried to do, a step at a time, until we eventually finish this." Bit by bit, Clinton is chomping away at the basic principles of a free enterprise health care delivery system that has delivered unquestionably the best health care available in the world today. The most important component of our present system is patient choice, and that is first on the chopping block for Clinton.

In an article appearing in the *New Republic* on January 19, 1998, author Jonathan Chait laments that the strategy seems to be working despite warning signals from the Republican leadership in the Congress. "It is clear that these initiatives are a Trojan Horse for implementing the once-defeated Clinton plan," Senate Majority Leader Trent Lott and

Majority Whip Don Nickles wrote in a memo to fellow Senators.

Yet, it is the Republicans who are getting thrashed by an effective spin-control machine at the White House, and now most Americans incorrectly believe that much of the Clinton plan will actually be good for the health care system. Chait observes "Kennedy-Kassebaum and Kiddiecare eventually sailed through virtually without public opposition, and Clinton's Bill of Rights (for patients) is registering Mother Theresa-like approval levels in opinion polls."

In Washington, approval ratings are the mother's-milk of politicians, and many critics run for cover when they look at the Clinton approval ratings. But masked behind these signs of public approval is the ugly fact that Americans are actually separating their view of Bill Clinton the likeable man from their actual strong disapproval with many of his key programs.

For the Republicans, it is a strange irony that they are probably responsible for Clinton's high approval ratings, since most Americans trust that Clinton will not be able to activate his liberal agenda with a conservative Congress watching his every move.

The problem with such thinking is that it is just plain wrong. Clinton can and is getting much of his agenda passed; he's just doing it more slowly, more effectively, and with little media attention.

Here's what that could mean to every senior

citizen in America:

Government control of who your doctor is going to be.

Make no mistake, this is the cornerstone of the Clinton plan for socializing medicine in America. It means that some faceless bureaucrat in Washington will be deciding who your doctor is going to be, and how much care you will be getting no matter what your real health needs are.

I'm not talking about reasonable restraints on cost. The Clinton plan simply strips consumers of choice in any part of their health care experience. Clinton has recruited an ultra-liberal group of extremist doctors, who call themselves Physicians for a National Health Program (PNHP), to try to sell his medical snake oil. For example, PNHP has published a series of questions and answers in which they lay out their liberal socialized medicine agenda. They claim a national health insurance program is not "socialized medicine," but rather is "socialized insurance." Is there a difference? Of course not. It's just fancy rhetorical footwork designed to mislead patients from the harsh truth about socialized medicine. The Clintons are trying to mislead people to believe that you can separate who controls the payment for services from the physician who actually delivers those services, as though the physician is completely independent. It is pure, unadulterated poppycock, and they know it.

If you can choose who your doctor is, you at least have the chance to develop an ongoing relationship with that doctor. He or she will know who you are, what your health history is, and what health problems you have had in the past. With this so-called "socialized insurance," however, you will be told which doctor you are assigned to, and that doctor will be told what kind of care they will authorize for you. You can bet that care will be the cheapest and most limited possible. That kind of health care system will not consider the kind of care you need. In fact, they will tell you what kind of care you are going to get, and you will just have to accept their judgment. It doesn't sound like the kind of health care system you want to have, does it?

Sadly, it gets even worse.

We can simply look to our neighbor in Canada, which has a socialized medicine system, to see what is in store for us under this Clinton health care scheme. It is not a pretty picture, but you can put yourself right in the middle of it if Bill and Hillary Clinton have their way.

Canadians cannot choose a doctor, they are assigned one. When they have a health problem, they are put on a waiting list unless it is a dire emergency. Even then, if the procedure is not life threatening, patients are put in the "queue" for scheduling of hospital procedures. All of that means one thing: the bureaucracy is making all of the choices, not the patient and the doctor.

Can you imagine the discomfort, pain and suffering patients must experience while waiting months, or even a year or more, for needed gall bladder surgery, a heart bypass operation, or even just cataract surgery?

Then there is the sad fact that socialized medicine systems typically resort to rationing of health care services. That means older and sicker patients are often excluded from receiving life-saving medical treatments.

Proponents of the Canadian health care system point to other countries and say their system is better. It's true, the Canadian system is better than the socialized system in Great Britain, where the waits for doctor appointments are longer, doctors have more patients to take care of, and the queue for getting into a hospital for a non-emergency procedure is longer. Wealthy Canadians just go to Seattle, Detroit, Buffalo or Boston to receive their medical care.

But Canada is quickly on its way to replicating the Great Britain model of health care delivery because they are both socialized medicine programs. None of the advantages of a free market system will ever be a part of those health care systems.

Great Britain does have an interesting twist to health care delivery they do not like to advertise. If you can afford it, you can purchase your own health care insurance, or buy your own health care services from non-government doctors or hospitals. There are no long waits and no rationing of care for these private health care providers because they are competing against one another to win the business of those who want to pay for private health care services. This private health care system is available only to the rich, because everyone has to pay taxes to support the socialized medical delivery system. The wealthy Britains simply pay double because they can afford it, and they get the care they need.

Americans have less freedom in health care choices today than patients in socialized medicine in Great Britain.

I know this statement seems unbelievable. It should be unbelievable. Yet, it constitutes the fundamental reason why the Clinton health care plan is such a huge fraud on all Americans. U.S. Senator Jon Kyl of Arizona correctly points out that "people in Great Britain with socialized medicine actually have more freedom and more choices in health care than are currently allowed senior citizens of the United States."

Senator Kyl points out that when you turn 65, you may well get a notice that your major medical health insurance plan is dropping you because you are now eligible for Medicare. It does not matter that you may have liked that plan, that it had good coverage, or that you have been seeing the same doctor in your small town or in your neighborhood for decades.

Worse, what if you are a diabetic and you have been given a referral from a friend to a doctor who is a specialist in treating diabetics? When you visit that doctor and the nurse assistant asks what your insurance company is, and you reply that it is Medicare, will it surprise you that the nurse may well then say, "I'm sorry, but the doctor does not participate in Medicare"? It happens to thousands of Medicare patients every year, and more and more doctors are opting out of Medicare because they are just fed up with the maze of restrictions imposed by government health care bureaucrats.

Now, here's the clincher. What if you still wanted to be treated by this doctor and informed the nurse you would pay for the services yourself? What if the nurse then told you that you could not pay personally for these services because the doctor would be charged with Medicare fraud and barred from Medicare reimbursement for two years if he or she treated you?

That is not some draconian story from a far-out science fiction novel. It is the rule of law in the United States today.

The Clinton Administration wants to make sure their brand of socialized medicine cannot be circumvented. These horrible regulations actually took effect on January 1, 1998 and provide that doctors will be kicked out of the Medicare system for two years for accepting payment directly from their patients who are Medicare beneficiaries for any medical service covered by Medicare.

If doctors do accept direct payments, they are required to submit a report to the Health Care Financing Administration in Washington that they have accepted payments directly from a Medicare eligible patent. This notice will then trigger a two-year suspension of any Medicare payments to that doctor for services delivered to Medicare patients.

When you turn 65 in America, you lose your freedom of choice. That's unfair and, frankly, un-American.

These regulations are being challenged in the courts, but the underlying problem is that this Administration will keep coming back to the basic philosophy of total government control of your health care. Even if this unfair and onerous regulation is removed, Bill and Hillary will find another way to do exactly the same thing.

Senator Kyl tried to fix this problem with legislation called the "Medicare Freedom to Contract Act." This legislation was added to the FY1998 budget by a vote of 64-35 in the U.S. Senate. Then, the Clinton Administration swooped in and threatened to veto the entire budget bill if the Kyl amendment were not stripped out.

Facing a government shutdown, the Congress had to allow Hillary Clinton to win that battle. The sad, unescapable fact is that Bill and Hillary Clinton cannot allow patients to have choices, because that is not a part of their twisted view of the value of a socialized government health care plan.

The American health care system is not perfect, but it is far better than the cynical and punitive socialized health care system envisioned by Bill and Hillary Clinton. I will be addressing in Chapter 6 of this book some improvements in our system that are possible without adopting such radical changes as favored by the Clintons.

The great fraud promoted by Bill and Hillary Clinton is that socialized medicine will be better for all Americans. The truth is it will be worse for practically all.

James Thurber's mother kept Muggs, the family dog, around even when he had the nasty habit of biting people. The Clinton health care plan is doing the same thing, but its bite is hard and potentially fatal to any hope senior citizens may have for preserving their freedoms in health care choices. Like Muggs, it may not be well, but it is indeed terribly strong.

FRAUD #2:

SENIOR VOTERS CARE ONLY ABOUT SOCIAL SECURITY AND MEDICARE

Individual Members of the U.S. Congress think they can win the support of older Americans by talking exclusively about Social Security and Medicare, and that's it. The idea that seniors care about only these two issues is an unfair and outdated political stereotype. However, this political stereotype permeates Congressional thinking, negatively impacting the quality of life for America's seniors. The thought that senior citizens' political concerns are limited to Social Security and Medicare issues is a fraud, and it demands to be corrected.

In a comprehensive poll conducted among a nationwide sample of more than 2,000 senior citizens across America, seniors identified eliminating government waste as the top priority on their list of important issues facing the country today. That was followed by their concern with the deterioration of ethics and morality in government, and the third most important issue to America's seniors was fighting crime.

Social Security, while important, was the fifth most important concern among seniors, just behind a concern about crooked politicians in elected office. Medicare was much further down the list.

Memo to Congress: wake up.

When seniors were asked which issues were important enough to take action on (defined as calling or visiting their Congressman, or donating money to groups that advocate for them), seniors ranked the following issues in order of importance:

ISSUE	One of Most Important Issues	A Very Important Issue	A Somewhat Important Issue	Not a Very Important Issue	A Very Unimportant Issue
Eliminate Wasteful Spending	38 %	58 %	3 %	1 %	1 %
Ethics and Morality in Government	36 %	56 %	6 %	1 %	1 %
Crooked Politicians	34 %	58 %	6%	2 %	n/a
Freedom to Choose Your Own Doctor	34 %	57 %	8 %	1 %	n/a
Protecting Your Social Security Benefits	33 %	57 %	8 %	1 %	1 %

Seniors want the government to eliminate wasteful spending, to restore ethics to government and get rid to crooked politicians, and they want the freedom to choose their own doctor in rankings of importance just ahead of protecting their Social Security benefits. Make no mistake, older Americans are concerned about Social Security and Medicare because those issues have a direct impact on their pocketbook, but they are equally concerned about issues that affect the quality of life for every American.

William Richter, assistant professor of international studies at Kansas State University, reports in *Collegian Magazine* that politicians "focus a tremendous amount of their political issues around what public opinion polls say. Politicians certainly want to know how salient an issue is, and what position people are taking." Most important, according to Richter, "Politicians need a quantifiable measurement of how their constituents feel about a subject."

There are two problems with the present view politicians have about interests seniors have in public policy issues. First, seniors are pigeon-holed into being concerned only about Social Security and Medicare because they have allowed themselves to be pigeon-holed. Second, politicians want to keep older Americans in a position where they have to address only those two issues to define themselves for senior voters.

Seniors are going to have to break these inaccurate stereotypes by speaking out clearly on those issues they are concerned about, and letting politicians know in no uncertain terms they will not be ignored.

Just look at the issue that ranked number one as the most important issue to seniors in a poll conducted by The Seniors Coalition: government waste. There is a good reason to be concerned, because government waste and mismanagement is presently out of control. The Citizens Against Government Waste publishes what they call the *Pig Book* every year. Here are some examples from the *1998 Pig Book* that were added to the budget without any competitive bidding or without the Senate receiving any request for the money from the Institute of Museum and Library Sciences:

- ◆ **$4,000,000** for projects to "use the resources of libraries and children's museums to provide innovative learning opportunities for at-risk children." The conference notes "urge" that the Children's Museums in Baltimore, Maryland; Boston, Massachusetts; and Philadelphia, Pennsylvania, receive the funding.

- ◆ **$1,930,000** for projects in Pennsylvania, home state of the Senate Labor/HHS/ Education Appropriations Subcommittee Chairman Arlen Specter (R-Pa.): $1,130,000 to maintain and interpret a historical collection of notes at the medical library of the College of Physicians in Philadelphia and $800,000 for a "one-of-a-kind historical library in Pennsylvania's anthracite coal region to assist in cataloguing and historic preservation of detailed information regarding miners' compensation and occupational records, geological studies, maps, newspaper clips and more than 8,000 photographs."

- ◆ **$1,000,000** for a demonstration project to

"provide interactive communications via the Internet to the information resources available between universities and their satellite campuses, community colleges and public, school and special libraries, and other entities" in the state of Senate appropriator Conrad Burns (R-Mont.). The Senate report "urges" that the money be sent to the Montana information consortium, which includes the University of Montana and Montana State University.

♦ **$1,000,000** to digitize the card catalog for the New York Public Library.

All of these projects are pork in the Labor/HHS/ Education Appropriations Bill, and they do not create jobs, move people off welfare rolls, or educate anyone. The only achieved result: to waste scarce tax dollars.

Sadly, these examples are only the tip of an iceberg that drags down a titanic federal budget. Here are several more examples of pork cited by the Citizens Against Government Waste that were added to this bill and, very importantly, were never requested in the Budget:

♦ **$24,798,000** added by the House for Health Professions' Centers of Excellence. (The Centers of Mediocrity received no funding this year.)

♦ **$3,798,000** added by the House for general dentistry residencies.

♦ **$1,000,000** added by the Senate for the "establishment of a center to provide in-state laboratory testing for businesses and training for high school graduates in the use of scientific testing equipment and techniques" in the state of Senate Labor/HHS/Education Appropriations subcommittee member James Jeffords (R-Vt.)

♦ **$1,000,000** added by the Senate for "a project similar to the ACCESS program at Prairie View A&M University" in the state of Senate Labor/HHS/Education Appropriations subcommittee member Kay Bailey Hutchison (R-Texas).

♦ **$500,000** added by the Senate for the University of Hawaii Center on the Family in the state of Senate appropriator Daniel Inouye (D-Hawaii).

♦ **$500,000** added in conference for the National Health Museum. The initial appropriation is for the establishment of a commission appointed by the President and House and Senate Leadership to study the museum proposal and develop a master plan.

The crushing weight of this pork, with all of the rest of it riddled throughout the Federal Budget, amounts to cruel robbery from every taxpayer. This same Congress sees a reason to make steep cuts in Medicare, creates unjustified arguments for reformulating the consumer price index to cut the size of the cost-of-living adjustments for Social

Security beneficiaries, and refuses to eliminate the earnings limits and estate taxes that take so much money from seniors' pockets.

Is it any wonder that government waste ranks as the number one concern of seniors? Is it any wonder that seniors rank concerns about government ethics and crooked politicians just a little higher than they do protecting their Social Security benefits? This pork is a fraud on taxpayers, and seniors have the right to be recognized for their opposition to such waste in government.

It is not surprising that politicians pigeon-hole seniors into the "Social Security/Medicare" box. The media plays a large role in the problem with narrow stories about seniors. When is the last time you saw a story about an issue seniors were concerned about that didn't focus on Social Security or Medicare? One of the largest so-called senior advocacy groups, AARP, spends a lot of time talking about how they work hard to protect Social Security and Medicare. Yet, when you look at the legislative priorities of AARP, there is example after example where AARP has advocated public policies that hurt seniors and all consumers in America. It is actually not surprising this is the case. AARP has to work hard to protect the extensive business relationships they have with various benefit providers from which they receive millions of dollars, but they also have to protect their biggest source of money: the United States Government. You will learn more about AARP and its fraud on seniors in Chapter 3 of this book.

Another well-known senior advocacy group, the National Committee to Preserve Social Security and Medicare, does exactly what its name implies: it focuses almost exclusively on Social Security and Medicare. When a Member of Congress or his or her staffer hears from lobbyists from these organizations, the myopic stereotype about seniors is reinforced.

Many staffers on Capitol Hill complain that the information they receive about seniors' concerns is too tightly focused on Social Security and Medicare; they say they desire a better profile of senior constituents. In other words, they want to know what the hot-buttons are for senior voters.

Seniors over 65 constitute the largest voter block in the electorate. Why? Because in many cases, younger people do not bother to even register to vote, let alone trudge to the voting booth on election day. But senior citizens take the time, consistently turning out in huge numbers as compared to other age cohorts in the general population.

Yet despite a disproportionately strong voice at the ballot box, our elected representatives have yet to seriously listen to the wide range of seniors' concerns. Seniors should stretch beyond the ballot box to communicate these concerns more profoundly to elected officials. Unless seniors convince Congress that they are more than a "two-issue" electorate, seniors will remain political doormats, placated by a lot of high-sounding rhetoric about Social Security and Medicare reforms.

Seniors can make a dramatic change in the

public issues debates simply by getting more involved in politics. There are a number of tips for doing this in the final chapter of this book, but here are some general suggestions for actions you can take today:

♦ **Call your Congressman and Senators today.** You can call your Congressman's local district office and register your opinion on any issue you choose. There is a trick to getting to the right staff person, so be certain to read the "Solutions" chapter at the end of this book. If the call is a toll-call, check for a toll-free number to reach your Congressman. If your Congressman's office does not have a toll-free number, mention that fact when you call the office to voice your opinion.

♦ **Write your Congressman and Senators.** What you write to your Congressman is important, and it will be read. If you are asked to send in a petition on an issue you agree with, by all means send it in. Petitions deliver powerful messages on Capitol Hill, and many Congressman will show up at a "photo-op" event just to get their picture taken with the huge stacks of petitions you have helped build. Individual letters are also important because they are used by Congressional staffers to gauge public opinion of constituents. Be sure to ask that your Congressman or Senator send a response to your letter.

♦ **Attend Town Hall Meetings.** Most

Congressmen hold community or "Town Hall" meetings to meet with their constituents. These meetings are typically used for the Congressman to tout their own legislative achievements, but you can go and express an opinion and ask questions. You should do it as often as you can; be sure to stand up and speak when you get there. These events are democracy at work, and you have the right to be heard. If your Congressman tries to change the subject, or he or she does not answer your question, just politely interrupt them and ask them to respond to your specific question. If you try it, you'll find it works.

♦ **Contribute to effective senior lobbying groups.** There are a number of senior advocacy groups in Washington who really do represent your views. When you find one, make contributions you can afford because they can deliver the message with great power. This book is published by one of the best senior advocacy groups, The Seniors Coalition, the only seniors group ranked by the prestigious *Roll Call* newspaper in Washington among the ten most effective lobbying groups on Capitol Hill. Your contribution, when joined by tens of thousands of others, forms the basis for the kind of high-powered lobbying campaign that you need to counter those who would oppose senior issues.

There's more you can do, and I strongly encourage you to carefully read the "Solutions" chapter where you will find more political action tips. In the meantime, get involved and put those Congressmen's feet to the fire. Seniors are a lot more than just Social Security and Medicare.

FRAUD #3:

AARP REPRESENTS SENIORS AND THEIR VIEWS TO THE U.S. CONGRESS

The American Association of Retired Persons (AARP) parades itself as the premiere senior advocacy group in America and claims that any senior who wants his views made known to the United States Congress should immediately join AARP. This is one of the biggest frauds on America's seniors today.

AARP is actually a huge benefits corporation that uses its members to justify receiving nearly $100 million in taxpayer dollars from various federal programs. The lobbying activities of AARP often work directly against the interests of seniors and support programs that cut benefits and increase costs and taxes for seniors. How AARP managed to construct this scheme and artifice to defraud America's seniors is a complex story of an organization that was built on providing an overpriced insurance policy for seniors. In this chapter we will examine those activities AARP has engaged in that are shockingly counter to the interests of seniors.

If there is an issue that provides a peephole into the murky legislative agenda for AARP, it is taxes. Despite clear membership data demonstrating that AARP members tend to be active retirees — many have launched a second career and are working taxpayers — AARP promotes every tax increase and opposes virtually every effort to cut taxes on working Americans. Worse, AARP is a champion advocate for increases in property taxes proposed in state legislatures across America. AARP has actively supported these tax increases nearly without exception even though the increased property taxes can force seniors on fixed incomes out of their homes because they cannot afford the property tax increases. In 1978, AARP was an active opponent to California's Proposition 13, legislation which limited property taxes to 1 percent of property values, and when it passed gave real relief to seniors on fixed incomes. Just a couple of years later, AARP joined a successful effort to defeat California's proposed cuts in property taxes by as much as 50 percent.

This pro-tax agenda is replicated in state after state where AARP lobbies hard to increase taxes and consistently fights attempts to limit or reduce taxes. How AARP justifies its continued efforts to undermine important issues like these to seniors who are misled into thinking that it really will protect seniors' economic positions remains a mystery.

On health care reform, AARP distinguished its anti-senior agenda in 1989 by pushing for the passage of the Medicare Catastrophic Care Act. This ill-conceived bill passed through the Congress easily and imposed one of the biggest Medicare Part B premium increases on seniors in the history of the program. This issue, which was of critical importance to Medicare beneficiaries, defines AARP and its philosophy. AARP continued to vigorously oppose the successful efforts of The Seniors Coalition, which was newly-formed to fight the steep premiums contained in the Medicare Catastrophic Care Act. When the Act was repealed in late 1989, AARP fell strangely silent in talking about the issue with its members.

AARP was also an early and vocal supporter of the Clinton health care reform package, which was nothing more than socialized medicine for all Americans. AARP's leaders persisted in actively lobbying for the Clinton plan even though it was clear that America's seniors were opposed to those provisions in it which undermined the services available to seniors. Worse, AARP was one of the leading participants in the secret meetings held in the White House to actually construct this government takeover of the health care delivery system. White House staffers, including First Lady Hillary Rodham Clinton, saw AARP as an absolutely essential shill consumer group they could use to justify support from seniors.

Critics of AARP claim that when AARP takes a position that appears to be detrimental to seniors' interests, it is because of self-serving decisions designed to actually increase revenues to AARP as an organization. In the case of the Clinton health care reform package, AARP was simply earning its annual payments of nearly $100 million in taxpayer-funded federal grants. It does not seem to matter much that these positions actually erode the financial well-being of their members, but only that AARP's financial bottom line is secure. Can there be a more compelling conflict of interest?

AARP's single largest source of money from the federal government is an ongoing grant from the Department of Labor/Employment Training Administration's Senior Community Service Employment Program. That single program brings in over $50 million to AARP coffers. Other grants from the Environmental Protection Agency's Senior Environmental Employment Program, the Treasury Department/Internal Revenue Service's Tax Counseling for the Elderly Program, and the Centers for Disease Control round out a pretty hefty package of federal tax dollars pouring into AARP bank accounts. How could AARP dare oppose any program offered by the Administration and its traditional liberal supporters in the Congress, and in the process risk being perceived to be biting the hand that feeds it?

Conflicts of interests have apparently never been a problem for AARP. While they are pushing higher property taxes that force seniors on fixed incomes out of their homes, they are using federal grants to fund studies that criticize seniors for failing to properly plan for costs they will encounter in retirement, including the costs of keeping their own homes. How could a senior anticipate that the organization they thought was protecting their financial interests would actually be a key player with the tax-and-spend liberals to send property taxes skyrocketing? As long as there are seniors having to give up their homes, AARP has its perfect issue by which it can seek funds to study with a federal grant.

Among members and staffers on Capitol Hill, AARP is viewed as a strongly liberal organization that is in lock-step with those who believe in big tax-and-spend government programs. Liberals who develop legislative strategies that involve using consumer groups to push for some leftist legislative agenda always list AARP as strong supporters. AARP legislative staffers are regularly included in liberal strategy sessions where they lay out plans to expand government programs and drive taxes up.

On the issue of private contracting by Medicare beneficiaries with their personal doctors, AARP claims it is opposed to allowing such freedoms because of the high risk of fraud. AARP points to a recent Health and Human Services Inspector General's report that Medicare loses $23 billion a year to fraudulent claims. How payment fraud can be attached to seniors who want to contract with a doctor privately to perform some medical procedure that is not going to be paid by Medicare remains one of life's perplexing mysteries. If anything, allowing seniors the freedom to go outside of Medicare to pay for their own health care because they choose to do so could only save Medicare money. Some Medicare beneficiaries complain that the allowance for hearing aids under Medicare does not deliver the quality of hearing aid product they could get if they paid for better quality hearing aids themselves. That is a choice of the beneficiary that he or she should be free to make; but under the AARP-supported private contracting law, it is illegal unless the doctor then agrees not to participate in any Medicare reimbursements for at least two years. This bill hurts every senior, but private contracting is a big issue to the liberals. And AARP has to do their bidding, no matter how embarrassing.

It is important to note that often AARP is just as crucial to the liberals if it doesn't take a position on an issue, even in the face of clear evidence that the enactment of the law or policy would harm the interests of seniors. In 1993, senior Democrats insisted AARP not alert its members about the provision in Clinton's deficit-reduction bill that raised taxes on high-income individuals who receive Social Security. By not fighting in that battle, AARP allowed the liberals to win in their first step to tax all Social Security beneficiaries not under the poverty line. That onerous tax increase on seniors passed by a single vote in the Congress.

The real business of AARP is the benefits it offers to members. But the shameless conflicts that permeate the legislative agenda also carry over to the benefits programs as well. Make no mistake, the stakes are huge for AARP. The organization raked in over $200 million in revenue from benefit providers AARP either owns or endorses. In the complex world of non-profit finances, AARP likes to call these revenues "royalties." But an extensive Internal Revenue Service audit showed AARP's level of management and involvement in the administration of these benefits was far greater than allowed by law, and imposed a huge $135 million fine on AARP for nonpayment of taxes on business income from its benefit program. The U.S. Postal Service also fined AARP $5,600,000 for illegally using its non-profit mailing permit to mail millions of solicitations to seniors for its insurance programs.

Here's the astounding part of this whole sordid story for AARP. With all of that history of tax evasion and illegal use of their non-profit mailing permit, AARP recently announced it was joining forces with the FBI and various State attorney generals to fight telemarketing fraud. Is there a better example of the fox guarding the chicken coop?

In a report justifying this alliance, note was taken that "During the Great Depression of the 1930s, hobos would leave a secret mark on the gate or doorway of a house where they got a handout to let other transients know they could expect help." These hobos were equated to the "people who run telephone marketing scams selling their lists to people who were targeted successfully so other telemarketers can cash in on careless and gullible customers." AARP has also volunteered to set up a group of 5000 volunteer AARP members to watch for illegal mailings to senior citizens who might be sent unsolicited letters. Is this the same AARP that was fined millions for postal fraud for sending illegally mailed and unsolicited insurance promotional packages to seniors?

Equally important, some attention should be given to the insurance product AARP was hawking, even if it had been mailed legally. AARP sells about 6,500,000 health and long-term care insurance packages through mail solicitations every year. Another 1,700,000 seniors buy AARP casualty coverage in auto and home policies. Yet, *Money* magazine rated the nine different types of AARP offered insurance as "decent to simply dreadful." *Money* also rated the AARP hospital indemnity plan as a "flat out waste of money." The conclusion offered by the *Money* analysts: "No matter how old you are, stay away." Yet, AARP is going to review telemarketing and unsolicited mail from companies offering similar services?

The last time I looked, even liberal judges don't assign bank robbers to perform their community service working in a bank. Yet, AARP just puts on its happy face and acts as though it has never had a problem in this area. You can bet they love the opportunity to screen the mail of seniors, particularly to refer solicitations from other competing senior advocacy groups to state and federal regulators.

The hypocrisy of AARP's leadership is found in a publication in which AARP responds to member questions about whether competing groups who solicit contributions with mailings are legitimate. AARP trashes the competitors and concludes with the ominous warning that "to put it rather bluntly, the objective of many organizations purporting to represent older Americans is simply to raise money." If one were standing at AARP headquarters listening to such a tortured explanation, it might well be difficult to hear the words over the deafening "cha-chinging" of the cash registers.

Here is one final example of how enmeshed and complicated a conflict of interest can be with the AARP benefit programs and legislative priorities. In early 1996, AARP announced it planned to begin licensing its name as a "seal of approval" to health maintenance organizations that meet its standards. This new initiative was not designed to be some sort of quality review of existing programs for AARP members to guide consumers to the best plans. In fact, AARP planned to solicit bids from HMOs who wanted this seal of approval in 15 or 16 different regional markets. These "seal of approval" designations were for sale.

The HMO program folded neatly into the Clinton health care plan which would force seniors into managed care plans and strip them of the right to choose their own doctors. AARP's legislative team encouraged the movement into the new money-making HMO endorsements as a perfect marriage between AARP's legislative agenda and its benefit program. More accurately, it was a perfect and clear conflict of interest. In December 1997, AARP had to announce that it had put this program on "indefinite hold" because the HMOs it was trying to affiliate with blew the whistle on AARP's requirement that the HMOs pay a $20 monthly royalty for every member enrolled in the program. That would surely help to give impetus for AARP to push a little harder for the mandates for managed care being promoted by liberals who are attempting to pass the Clinton health care plan incrementally.

AARP is a business, and a big one at that, masquerading as a non-profit advocacy group concerned about a vulnerable and fragile membership. When AARP looks at an issue, it has to check with both its liberal mentors on Capitol Hill and its accountants to see how it will impact their bottom line. Then it has to make certain it will not offend the disbursers of the federal grant monies that are such a large part of AARP's revenues. It is no wonder that so many seniors feel cheated by AARP when they get to know what their dues actually pay for. As an independent advocate for seniors' interests, AARP is a fraud.

FRAUD #4:

BRAND NAME DRUGS HAVE TO CHARGE MORE TO FUND NEEDED RESEARCH

Brand name drug companies claim they have to charge higher prices, even after their 20-year patent life has expired, in order to fund critically needed research. There can be no denial that drug therapies are the very best buy in American health care, but the argument about research is too big a pill to swallow. It is this "poster child" argument which the Congress of the United States continues to accept in one legislative battle after another. It is, however, a pernicious fraud on every patient, every health care professional, and every American.

Why would brand name drug companies engage in a systematic scheme to defraud the American public? The answer: billions and billions of dollars are at stake. In its quest to unfairly extend its monopoly pricing on brand name drug products, the pharmaceutical industry has consistently attempted to undermine the public confidence in generic drug products. When the story is fully exposed, the actions of these brand name drug companies will shock you.

In January 1998 the U.S. Food and Drug Administration (FDA) took the unprecedented step of issuing a public letter rebuking Dupont-Merck, a brand name drug company trying to keep a generic version of a popular blood thinning drug off the market, for its inaccurate public statements about the safety and effectiveness of the generic version that had been approved by the FDA. This letter sternly made the point that such claims are unjustified given the scientific testing required for generic products to obtain such approvals.

The cornerstone of the brand name strategy is to keep generic drugs off the market as long as possible. And when they are available on the market, these brand companies are working hard to undermine consumer and health care provider confidence in the safety and quality of generic drug products.

Here is a secret these brand companies would just as soon you didn't know at all: generic drugs are just as safe and effective as their brand name counterparts are, or the FDA would not allow them on the market. This fact is important to understand because everything the brand name drug industry does in its marketing after patent expiration is designed to have you believe otherwise.

There is only one standard for drug quality in the United States, and it applies to every drug manufactured in America whether a brand or generic.

The FDA establishes and enforces these scientific standards. A generic drug is not only required to undergo rigorous tests to prove that it precisely matches the chemical composition of the brand product, but it must also be tested on human subjects to prove it exactly matches the brand name's absorption of the drug into a patient's bloodstream. Finally, a generic drug must have the same clinical therapeutic effect as the brand drug on the patient. After passing this extensive battery of scientific tests, the FDA then certifies that the generic drug is an exact match of the brand product. These generic products are assigned an "A" rating by FDA to affirm they have met all of the required tests.

The brand name drug industry fears generic competition for a simple, basic reason. Why would any consumer pay a higher price for a product that is just as safe, just as effective, and yield precisely the same result? They won't, and therein lies the motive for the brand industry to defraud the American public.

A recent event illustrates very well the depth of the problem for American consumers. In late 1994, a Congressional staffer made a simple clerical error in the drafting of implementing legislation for the United States' participation in an international treaty known as the General Agreement on Tariffs and Trade, commonly referred to as "GATT." This treaty, among other things, was designed to standardize the patent periods on intellectual property among all signatory nations to a period of 20 years from the date of submission of the product to the patent authority.

Under U.S. patent law prior to the GATT, patents were granted for a period of 17-years from the date of approval of the patent. It was the intention of negotiators of the treaty that all products would be covered, including pharmaceutical products. These negotiators recognized that many competitors had already been preparing to enter the market with generic copies of patented products before the treaty was enacted. It would be unfair to such individuals or companies who had made substantial investments in manufacturing capability to suddenly have the rug pulled out from under them. So the treaty had a transition period to protect those companies.

The mistake made by the Congressional staffer in drafting the technical language of the implementing bill omitted a key phrase recognizing the requirement of generic drug manufacturers in the United States to receive approval of the FDA prior to entering the marketplace. The error essentially blocked the transition provision of GATT for generic drug manufacturers in America even though every other industry in every other country could avail itself of this protection.

Congress makes such mistakes every day in its legislative process, and they are routinely addressed in what are called "technical corrections" bills. Interestingly, this error was discovered by an attorney working for Glaxo, Inc., who saw how his client could block generic competition under strict interpretation of poorly written language in the implementing bill. That attorney was later quoted in *Business Week* magazine, calling it a "Eureka Moment."

A "Eureka Moment" indeed. That mistake was worth more than $6 billion in windfall profits to the brand name drug industry. For Glaxo, it allowed for an unearned, unanticipated, and unwarranted patent extension for its immensely popular anti-ulcer drug, Zantac®. For Zantac® alone it was a $3.2 billion windfall profit over the extended patent period. Attach another 112 or so products and another $3 billion, and its total added up to a blockbuster mistake.

But there is no way that Congress would allow consumers to be ripped-off for that $6 billion simply because of a clerical error by one of its committee staffers, right?

Wrong. In the world of Washington politics, money talks and walks, and with an overflowing political action committee budget and virtually every lobbyist in town on the payroll, Glaxo pulled out all of the stops to win this jackpot.

The plot thickens considerably at this point. Glaxo won the support of one of the most powerful members of the U.S. Senate, Orrin G. Hatch of Utah. Senator Hatch is from my home state, and I was certain that he would stand up for families and the elderly who would be hit the hardest by this unfair patent extension. Vulnerable seniors on fixed incomes are not the only losers in Utah. Young, large families are the rule in Utah, and those families and the hundreds of thousands of seniors are among the hardest hit economically because they had to purchase the exorbitantly priced brand name drugs, a price that was protected on the market longer because of the GATT mistake. And seniors, because of age-related chronic disease and illness, are the highest volume purchasers of these needed drug products. But Orrin Hatch sided with Glaxo, and unless you know the inner workings of Washington, you would never understand why he would turn his back on his constituents in this way.

When a patent expires on a brand product, the price for a therapeutically equivalent generic competitor is approximately 40 to 60 percent less than the price charged for the brand product. It was Senator Hatch who led the charge in 1984 for passage of the Drug Price Competition and Patent Term Restoration Act, commonly referred to as the "Hatch-Waxman Act," which created the structure for a generic drug industry to flourish. Since that time, consumers have saved literally billions of dollars over what they would have paid for brand name products. It is indeed ironic that Senator Hatch would switch sides so dramatically to protect a brand name drug company that places profits above consumer interests.

There are two possible explanations for Hatch's seemingly bizarre behavior. First, Glaxo had been a strong campaign supporter of Senator Hatch, doling out the maximum contribution to Hatch's various election efforts. Glaxo has also been an unusually strong supporter of the University of Utah. Over the past two decades Glaxo has given more than $20 million in unrestricted grants to the University of Utah, which is unprecedented in terms of proportional contributions the company has made to other educational research institutions who have no apparent ties to the company.

But those who know Hatch well claim that Glaxo's contributions to the University of Utah fulfilled a specific political need for Senator Hatch. Hatch was first elected to the Senate in 1976 after a hard-fought campaign in which Hatch was branded a "carpetbagger" because he had moved to Utah from his native state of Pennsylvania. Despite his win, Hatch was stung by the rejection of the insider "Salt Lake crowd" who built a culture around their loyalty to the University of Utah. Glaxo helped Senator Hatch buy his way into that lofty political circle by brokering these huge research investments into the University of Utah. To an outsider it may seem insignificant, but to Hatch it bought a source of political capital that has helped him to three subsequent election wins against some of those "Salt Lake crowd" insiders that would obviously been tougher without the largesse from Glaxo.

The second explanation for Hatch's unaccountable and surprising anti-consumer position is rooted in an interesting relationship Senator Hatch has with a former staffer, Tom Parry. In 1984, Tom Parry worked for the generic drug industry and

Hatch made a dramatic philosophical switch to give energy and momentum to the generic industry's efforts to pass legislation to allow for non-commercial testing of patented products so generic products could theoretically enter the market on the date of patent expiration. In 1996, when the GATT battle erupted, Tom Parry's lobbying firm had switched sides to work for Glaxo and a number of other brand name drug companies. In a recent lobbying disclosure report, Parry's lobbying firm also listed the likes of Pharmacia & Upjohn, Genentech, Hoffman-LaRoche, ICN Pharmaceuticals, Pfizer, Schering-Plough and the Pharmaceutical Research and Manufacturers of America, all huge brand name drug interests.

As in 1984 when he gave energy to Parry's generic industry clients, Hatch provided the energy and momentum in the GATT battle for the brand name drug companies to turn the tide in what should have been a routine fix for an innocent mistake made in the drafting of the GATT implementing legislation. The negotiators from the U.S. Trade Representatives Office testified before Congress that they had intended to protect generic drug companies; individual staffers who crafted the language acknowledged they had made a mistake in the way the language was written; and most in Congress admitted it was a mistake that should have been corrected.

The argument Hatch used to cover his economic abuse of seniors and families who were entitled to access to more reasonably priced generic drugs was that the windfall profit to the brand companies were critically needed to fund new research. That research would, in turn, produce breakthrough drug therapies that would save lives and improve the quality of life for patients who otherwise would suffer. That all sounds pretty good, doesn't it?

It was, of course, a well crafted lie.

Senator Hatch pointed his accusatory finger at the generic drug industry and unfairly denounced them for their "greed" in trying to deprive the brand industry of the research money it needed to benefit patients. It was, however, not the generic drug industry that would lose the money since they would eventually have access to the market after the unfair patents had expired. A delay in making money is different from losing money. The losers were American consumers who had to shell out hard-earned money for exorbitantly priced brand name drugs much longer than they should have.

The brand name drugs Hatch was defending had already enjoyed 17-years of patent life under U.S. patent law. The brand name manufacturers had not anticipated the GATT windfall extensions, so they had priced their product over the 17-year patent life to recover the research and development costs and their profits.

A study conducted in 1996 by the now-disbanded Congressional Office of Technology Assessment, of which Senator Hatch served on the Board, found that brand companies typically recovered the research and development costs in the first couple of years of the patent period, and the remaining 15 or so years were simply profit earners for the company. That study also revealed in detail the methods by which brand companies fund new drug research, little of which had to do with revenues generated from product sales.

In reality, the windfall profits won by Glaxo with their multi-million dollar lobbying campaign were ultimately used in a multi-billion dollar buy-out of a competing pharmaceutical company, Burroughs-Wellcome. Some research. Not one new product, just a lot of shifting of massive corporate wealth, mostly between cash-rich bank accounts and the pockets of their stockholders.

If Senator Hatch was caught red-handed in his duplicitous defense of Glaxo, he hasn't shown it. The brand name juggernaut continues unabated as they erect barrier after barrier for access to the market by the generic industry in what has become a literal blockade against generic competition.

The brand name drug industry relies upon the secrecy and complexity that shrouds the pharmaceutical industry to hide the truth from consumers. Let me give you just a few examples of how the brand industry gets away with their blockade of generic products from consumers.

♦ **Citizens Petitions.** There is a law that allows for citizens to submit a petition to the FDA if they feel there is some important public policy that would be served if the FDA were to make some regulatory decision. Brand name drug companies routinely submit Citizens Petitions in attempts to raise unfair questions about generic drug products that are under review by FDA. This is an abuse of the system, and it is done purely to slow down the approval of generic drugs so consumers will have to pay higher prices for the brand drugs. FDA is required under this law to investigate every issue raised in each Citizens Petition filing, and that takes valuable resources away from the Office of Generic Drugs that could be used for the review and approval of generic drugs for consumers.

♦ **Paragraph IV Certifications.** Pharmaceutical law provides that a patent holder can challenge a generic applicant if they believe the generic infringes on the rights of that patent holder. If a brand company challenges a generic application, the law provides that FDA cannot issue an approval for as long as 30 months while the issue is litigated in the courts. Brand companies have found this is an easy way to extend the life of their patents, so they file a lot of Paragraph IV challenges. They lose or withdraw the vast majority of these challenges, but they continue to rake in huge profits while the generic application is put on hold. In other words, consumers lose, brand companies win.

♦ **Limit Raw Material Access.** The only way generic companies can manufacture products is if they have the high-quality raw materials to make them. Brand companies sign long-term contracts with domestic raw material suppliers that restrict generic companies from buying them in the United States. Then, the brand companies use their ties to foreign affiliates to lobby their own governments to restrict exportation of these raw material supplies. United States patent laws allow generic manufacturers to import patented raw materials in order to conduct tests for their FDA application for that product. The brand companies subvert this law and block many generic products, sometimes for years beyond the patent expiration of the brand product, because it forces consumers to pay those unfair and inflated prices.

These are just a few of the tricks used by the brand industry to keep consumers from access to generic competition. It is a horribly scandalous rip-off that hurts every consumer, and it should be stopped. Here are a few examples about how dramatic the differences in price can be between the cost of a brand name drug and the generic competitor:

Brand	Generic	Strength	Brand Cost	Generic Cost	Consumer Savings
Tagamet ®	Cimetidine	400 mg	$160.98	$69.70	$91.28
Zantac ®	Ranitidine	150 mg	$107.92	$52.28	$55.64
Klonopin ®	Clonazepan	1 mg	$110.20	$48.43	$61.77
Darvocet-N ® 100	Propoxyphene Napsylate + Acetaminophen	100 mg 650 mg	$73.10	$28.53	$44.57

Reprinted with permission from The Seniors Coalition Advocate

These savings are dramatic on paper, but they really need to be put into context of those seniors who need these prescription drugs but live on limited fixed incomes. Often, it comes down to the awful choice as to whether seniors buy their medications or buy food they need to eat. Or, seniors have to choose between paying the rent or buying their medications. Brand name drug companies force consumers into impossibly tight corners when they block more reasonably priced generic competition from the pharmacy shelves.

These brand companies also spend tens of millions of dollars every year to convince our doctors that they should prescribe the brand drug rather than the generic. Think about that: these greedy brand drug companies want doctors to prescribe brand name drugs when there is a generic that is just as safe and just as effective. It's not about health, it's about money; money for those brand name drug giants who say research is their most important priority.

Those brand companies pay drug salesmen to fan out across the country to visit every doctor in

America who prescribes their product. We should have complete confidence when we have confidential conversations with our doctors that we will get the best advice and treatment. We don't. Many doctors prescribe the brand product because they feel a strong loyalty to those drug salesmen. It is a fair question to ask why, and the answer shows how deep the fraud goes.

Whenever a brand name drug company introduces a new product, they hold "educational" seminars to brief doctors on what the drug does for patients. These seminars are held in exotic locations, offer lots of free time for recreational activities like golf and tennis, and they essentially "bribe" our doctors to always prescribe the brand drug, even when a generic is available.

Recent statistics on prescribing patterns show that over 30 percent of prescriptions written by doctors where generics are available direct the pharmacist to dispense the brand product. The doctor writes on the prescription or checks a box that says "Brand Medically Necessary." As we all know, there is no medical or scientific justification to write any prescription as "Brand Medically Necessary."

It's a fraud on every fragile senior citizen and on every low-income family. It's a fraud on the Medicare and Medicaid programs which do not have the funds needed to cover eligible patient care because they spend so much on prescription medications. It's a fraud on every consumer in America, and it is past time that this fraud came to an end.

FRAUD #5:

SOCIAL SECURITY IS SAFE AND SECURE

Social Security is safe and secure.

If you don't believe it, just ask President Bill Clinton who commented on what was then the latest revisions to Social Security law on August 15, 1994.

> ". . . we are reinventing our government to streamline operations so that we can serve the American people better. . . It is proving that government can still work to improve people's lives. And now Social Security, we know, will work even better."

There are many who distrust Bill Clinton, and they think he will distort the truth about the security of Social Security in the same way he has misled the public about other matters. For those cynics, perhaps you can rely upon the words of John A. Svahn, who served as the Commissioner of Social Security from 1983 - 1986, and who talked of its solvency and security in 1985.

"It was more than just a President's signature put down that day. It was a sure sign that Social Security will remain as it should a program that will indeed keep its promises to generations to come."

Even Ronald Reagan offered his assurances at a signing ceremony on April 20, 1982 for changes in the law. The President expressed confidence in the stability of the Social Security system when he told Americans they could trust in the future.

"The changes in this legislation will allow Social Security to age as gracefully as all of us hope to do ourselves, without becoming an overwhelming burden on generations still to come. . . . And younger people can feel confident that Social Security will still be around when they need it to cushion their retirement."

The architect of the Social Security system, President Franklin Roosevelt, set forth the philosophical underpinnings of the government's commitment to Social Security when he gave his message to Congress in June, 1934.

"These three great objectives the security of the home, the security of livelihood, and the security of social insurance are, it seems to me, a minimum of the promise we can offer to the American people. They constitute a right which belongs to every individual and family willing to work . . . ."

These brave and forceful statements all have one thing in common: they constitute a clear and continuing fraud on the American people. They are, in their most benign form, simply statements of politicians who will do or say almost anything in their pursuit of approval from a distrustful and jaded electorate. These statements perpetuate the fundamental lie being told to generation after generation of Americans.

During the Great Depression, many public figures and politicians wanted the public to believe that the economic crisis was just another dip in the economic cycle that would shortly correct itself. Shortly after the stock market crash, this pablum of public pronouncements was particularly common.

On New Year's day 1930, Secretary of the Treasury Andrew Mellon stoically observed: *"I can see nothing in the situation which warrants pessimism."* President Herbert Hoover defiantly stated: *"Any lack of confidence in the economic future or the basic strength of business in the United States is foolish."*

The truth was harsh, and the lesson painful.

When President Roosevelt was elected in 1932, he proposed a program for economic security based on social insurance rather than welfare assistance. That concept changed the course of debate in the Congress, and paved the way for the enactment of a radical new approach to economic security for the elderly.

That same revolutionary thinking is now

surfacing in the Congress as a new concept for economic security for America's elderly enters the public policy arena. But in the interim, the Social Security system as we know it will not benefit from fundamental deception on the part of our leaders about its shortcomings.

The truth is, with the present funding formula set forth in law, the trouble in the system starts in less than ten years. It is true today that the government collects more in Social Security taxes than it pays out in benefits. That is only a temporary condition, with a large group of aging baby boomers ready to overload the system.

In 2005, the Trust Fund will start suffering from a decline in revenues, and by the year 2013, the current surplus will be replaced by deficits. In the year 2030, the Social Security Trust Fund will be bankrupt. The bankruptcy numbers will be staggering. In 2020, annual Social Security benefit payments will exceed deposits from payroll deductions by an estimated $232 billion, and continue the flood of red ink to a crippling $766 billion annual shortfall in 2030.

Politicians take great umbrage at the comparison of the present funding method for Social Security to a Ponzi scheme. Yet, it is difficult to read any commentary about the problems with the Social Security system without recognizing similarities between the two projects.

Charles Ponzi was a Boston investment banker who catapulted to prominence in the early months of

1920 when he promised fabulous rates of returns to investors in foreign postal coupons. Throughout the spring months, big money investors approached Ponzi with their hopes of investing in his scheme. Then, in August, the Ponzi Pyramid failed, and it brought down six Boston banks and stole the fortunes of thousands of investors.

The essence of the scheme was that Ponzi used the money he received from later investors to pay exorbitant rates of return to early investors. That provided strong incentives for more investors to pump more money into the scheme in the false hope they would receive the same inflated rates of return. This scheme works only as long as there is an ever-increasing number of new investors coming into the scheme to support the growing burden on other investors.

Supporters of the Social Security system's "pay-as-you-go" structure argue that it is fundamentally different from a Ponzi scheme because it maintains a rough balance between those paying into the system and those collecting from the system. However, whether it is just bad luck or a fundamental flaw, the future of the Social Security system is doomed for exactly the same reason Ponzi schemes always fail: too few dollars coming into the system to pay for more people collecting from it from earlier investments.

Another serious problem looming for Social Security is the investments that have been made in order to secure the availability of money when beneficiaries are entitled to withdraw funds they have invested. By law, Social Security can only invest in government securities, and that has provided a rate of return of about 2.3 percent after inflation.

Historically, the stock market has an average rate of return of 7 percent. The difference, compounded over decades, is enormous.

There was an interesting analysis that appeared in the *Dallas Morning News* in May, 1997, of what a couple entering the workplace in 1985 could have expected if their monies had been invested more prudently. If this couple earned the average U.S. income each year until retirement and invested the equivalent of the Social Security taxes in stocks with an average real return of only 4 percent (which is very low by historical standards), they would be in a far better position as compared to what they will receive under Social Security.

♦ They would have a cash balance in their account of $1.1 million at retirement.

♦ They would receive monthly benefits more than three times greater than they would under Social Security.

♦ If they chose to live solely off of the interest from the $1.1 million, they would receive more than under the present system.

♦ For workers who made a higher-income that the average U.S. wage, the monthly retirement income could be as much as $11,000 per month.

The existing Social Security system relies upon

current workers to pay the benefits of current retirees. When Congress enacted Social Security in 1935, there were about 37 workers for every retired person. Today, only three workers are available to support each Social Security beneficiary, and that will shrink to only about two workers for each retiree in just a few years.

Another major problem is that the money simply isn't there in the Trust Fund. There is a stack of IOUs from the government, and when those IOUs come due, the government is going to have to raise taxes to pay them back. Current projections contemplate Social Security payroll taxes will have to jump from the current 12.4 percent of pay to a minimum of 16.5 percent in 2030. Some more pessimistic projections push that rate to a whopping 37 percent of pay earned by a worker.

If that doesn't sound like a Ponzi scheme, then I don't know what would.

The only other obvious solution would be to drastically cut the benefits putting beneficiaries back into the days when poverty was the norm for older Americans.

Worse news for supporters of the present Social Security system is the lack of faith that young people have in the system. One public opinion poll found that more people believe in UFO's than believe Social Security will be available to them when they retire.

That brings us to the politicians.

In the past, people who made the decision to

run for public office had ingrained in them that it was political suicide to mess with Social Security. A new political reality has emerged now that so many average citizens are fully aware that Social Security is on the brink of bankruptcy.

It is now too risky for politicians to ignore this problem at the risk of their credibility.

But the solutions are still far too controversial for Congress to grab the problem and solve it. Whenever Congress faces such dilemmas, it reaches into its bag of political chicanery and pulls out a tried and true Congressional dodge, and that is exactly what it is doing to avoid confronting the tough choices in resolving the impending bankruptcy of the Social Security system. The dodge: the appointment of a Commission to study what should be done to solve the funding shortfall in the Social Security system. In the best of all worlds for the politicians, the Commission would have the authority to develop a solution and it would then become law absent an affirmative Congressional action to intervene and stop it. Sound familiar? That's precisely how Congress avoids the political firestorm in granting themselves their pay raises these days. They let a Commission do it, and you can bet they won't pass any legislation to stop a proposed pay increase. Unfortunately for the Congress, the problem is not quite that simple in salvaging a bankrupt Social Security system.

Congress presently addresses the problem by tinkering with the system just enough to push the day of disaster a little further into the future. They whittle away at the existing benefits to reduce the outlays to beneficiaries and forestall the day of reckoning. A perfect example of such tinkering is found in proposals to reduce the cost of living adjustment formula, commonly referred to as COLAs. These COLAs are based upon a complex formula of market basket items which comprise the annual consumer price index (CPI). Congressional budget cutters claim the CPI has been overstating the actual value of the inflation rate by at least two-tenths of a percentage point a year since 1987. An independent panel of economists put the error at 0.7 percent to 2 percent a year.

It is a politician's dream. Senator Patrick Moynihan of New York, normally more intellectual than the average Senator, jumps on this solution with gusto. Cutting the COLA by just 1 percent a year would deliver $281 billion in savings to the Trust Funds over seven years. That's fully one-third of the $894 billion that Republicans controlling the Congress claim is needed to balance the budget by 2002. When Congress is on the prowl for money, they get bi-partisan in a hurry. Senator Moynihan, a Democrat, says "We are at an impasse. We need money. I think this is the only way we can get out of this." Senator Moynihan is wrong.

The CPI is actually understated for seniors and poor families. The market basket of goods and services used to calculate the CPI fails to include the frequency and extent of medical services required by seniors, and the lack of funds to make any choices for goods available significantly understates the real CPI for seniors. For example, well-to-do people may be able to choose among a variety of supermarkets, but poor and elderly people simply don't have the mobility to get around that well. Seniors also lack access to easy transportation common to baby boomers. Merton Bernstein, an economist and law professor at Washington University in St. Louis, points out that seniors and poor families have to go to so-called convenience stores, so they "don't have the substitution effect." In addition, seniors often are unable to get to discount stores, which are "primarily a suburban institution," says Bernstein. "If you're stuck in the central cities, as an undue proportion of minority and elderly people are, you're out of luck."

Some economists suggest the CPI understates the senior CPI by as much as 1 percent annually.

But the issue in Washington is that Congress needs to find money to balance the budget, not spend more. The impetus for reforming the Social Security system is to cut spending rather than fairly deal with beneficiaries, thus placing a death grip on any economic argument. No matter how compelling, Congress is not willing to do the right thing and fairly adjust the COLA payment to accurately reflect the true CPI for seniors. Congress wants the money from slicing the COLA as a savings, and that's exactly what they got when the Bureau of Labor Statistics made an unfavorable adjustment to the CPI in April 1998. That change will reduce the COLA for Social

Security beneficiaries, and by 2001 will reduce the monthly payment by $20 per month, or a whopping $240 a year. If the CPI were fairly calculated for seniors to account for goods and services actually purchased by seniors, the CPI would be increased by as much as 2%, and that would increase monthly payments by nearly $60 a month, or $720 a year. When you look at what was unfairly done to seniors with the recalculation of the CPI, coupled with the true senior CPI, seniors are losing $80 a month in the year 2001, or an astounding $960 every year. And you can bet that Congress won't lift a finger to stop this unfair adjustment to the CPI for seniors.

Congress must move away from the present reliance on a pay-as-you-go system while protecting both the present beneficiaries and those who would not have had time to invest for their own retirement. Any transition period to some sort of Social Security system must allow new beneficiaries to invest a portion of their retirement funds in the stock market. The anemic returns from government securities are not capable of providing for future retirement needs. It is a system that needs changing, and those who participate are crying out for change.

A poll conducted by the well-known and respected CATO Institute in Washington found that 47 percent of seniors now favor moving to a privatization of the Social Security system, adding to the 69 percent of Americans overall who favor privatization. The Seniors Coalition conducted an extensive poll of its own members and non-affiliated seniors and found that 53 percent favored privatization.

The question is no longer whether we should allow for individual choice in using private investments for beneficiaries, but rather how we should construct such a system. Unfortunately, that is the issue that the Congress becomes totally paralyzed over. Making the change requires political courage, a quality lacking among today's Washington crowd.

Protection of existing beneficiaries must take the top priority. The U.S. government entered into a contract with America's seniors which it must honor. Social Security is not exclusively a retirement program, so the stakes for every American are very high. Forty percent of the 42 million people receiving Social Security benefits are not retired workers, they are the spouses and children of retired workers or are receiving disability or survivor benefits as the spouse, children, widow(er) or parents of retired, deceased, or disabled workers.

How important is Social Security to you and your family?

About 42 percent of men and 30 percent of women will die or become disabled before reaching their retirement years. About 98 percent of the children under 18 and their mothers or fathers (with children under age 16) can count on monthly cash benefits if a working parent dies. About four out of five men and women between 21 and 64 can count on monthly cash benefits if the wage earner becomes disabled.

The problem is that these Americans cannot depend upon a system that is about to collapse under the crushing weight of its own debt structure. America has shown an ability to adapt to new ideas and adopt creative solutions to problems just as difficult as this. Our ability to send a man to walk on the moon and bring him back was one of the greatest scientific achievements of the century. It required the government to amass the best group of scientists possible, to accept cutting-edge technologies and creative solutions to otherwise insurmountable problems. That same kind of problem-solving genius can and should be applied to solving the Social Security problem.

The most current Advisory Council on Social Security has proposed some relatively aggressive, albeit incremental changes to address the immediate problems. Six of the thirteen panelists, led by former Social Security Commissioner Robert Ball, believe the expanding elderly population can be best protected if the government invests up to 40 percent of the system's funds in stocks, which have historically yielded a return of about 10 percent, compared with about six percent from Treasury securities.

A second group of five of these panel members favors a system similar to Chile's where workers would create their own personal savings accounts with a large portion of the money they are required to pay in to the Social Security system.

The majority of these panelists, made up of many of the government bureaucrats who have been part of the system for so long, seem now only lukewarm to exploring these new, creative concepts.

America desperately needs to recommit itself to its moral duty to protect its senior citizens, and to honor its obligation to a Social Security system that working Americans were promised would be there in their retirement years. The Seniors Coalition motto states clearly that its mission is to protect the future America's seniors have earned. It could not be said any better than that.

Fraud #6:

Medicare:
Saved From Bankruptcy and Secure for the Future

One of the big political lies told virtually every year is that Medicare is now secure for the future. Then somehow, the very next year, Medicare is back in financial trouble and more pervasive and deeper program cuts have to be made. This huge lie constitutes fraud for every senior in America.

The problem with Medicare is not that it lacks money to pay claims for existing beneficiaries; rather, it is the future bulge of baby boomers that threatens to destroy the future of the system. Capitol Hill's attempted "fixes" aim to band-aid the forthcoming baby boomer crisis while wrongly wrapping a tourniquet around existing benefits.

On July 30, 1965, President Lyndon B. Johnson issued the first Medicare card to former President Harry Truman, the man who had first proposed the Medicare concept twenty years earlier. The event marked the advent of the Social Security

Administration's new authority to extend health coverage to almost every American aged 65 or older. Nearly 20 million beneficiaries enrolled in Medicare in the first 3 years of the program's enactment.

The need for such a program was evidenced in a survey conducted in 1956 by the U.S. Public Health Service which revealed that seven out of ten Americans over the age of 65 had no health insurance at all. Those who did have insurance faced steep and escalating premiums as they got older, high deductibles, and ever-changing benefit termination standards.

Today, Medicare now covers roughly 38 million Americans; 33 million aged 65 and over, and about 5 million under the age of 65 who are disabled. Medicare is a social insurance program that is funded primarily by payments made by beneficiaries during their working years. Those funds are supplemented today by payment of premiums for certain services and additional taxes levied upon the general population but dedicated for use by the Medicare system.

The funding for the Medicare Hospital Insurance Trust Fund, commonly referred to as Part A benefits, comes from a payroll tax of 2.9%, split evenly between employees and employers. A person who is self-employed pays the entire 2.9%. The Trust Fund pays for hospital stays for beneficiaries, less a deductible equal to about the cost of one day in the hospital.

Part B benefits are paid out of the Supplementary Medicare Insurance Trust Fund. This Trust Fund is financed with monthly premium payments by beneficiaries and contributions from general revenues of the federal government. These Part B benefits cover care by a physician and other health care providers outside of the hospital setting.

There can be no debate that the fundamental structure of Medicare needs to be overhauled in order to deal with the baby boomer problem. But instead of making those changes so they apply in the years when they are needed, the Congress shows political cowardice by administering a little first aid when major surgery is needed.

The harsh fact is that Medicare spending is projected to be significantly greater than the growth in the economy. The Congressional Budget Office predicts that over the next 10 years Medicare spending will increase by 8.8 percent annually juxtaposed against an economy that is expanding by only 4.7 percent a year. With the projected growth in baby boomer Medicare beneficiaries slated to hit in 15 years, those kinds of numbers are simply unsustainable. It means either drastic budget cuts in other programs in the Federal Government or significant tax increases.

The Congressional response to date is to keep ratcheting down the payments made for care to beneficiaries. It began in the early 1980s under President Ronald Reagan with the implementation of the Prospective Payment System (PPS). PPS merely put limits on what would be paid to hospitals for certain medical procedures provided to Medicare beneficiaries. Each physical and mental event requiring intervention was assigned a code, called a Diagnostic Related Group, or DRG, and a payment was assigned to that DRG.

The PPS was designed to strip the fat out of the health care delivery system in hospitals. The DRG payments were phased in over a period of years, gradually squeezing hospitals until they were forced to meet fairly tight reimbursement levels. While it was originally intended to be just a two or three year "transition" program to a payment system where each beneficiary would be assigned a specific amount of money for their health care each year to be paid to health care providers, the PPS system is still in effect today and there is no real prospect that it will be thrown on the scrap heap anytime soon.

There has been a lot of screaming from the hospital sector about payments being too small for the intensity of care provided to Medicare beneficiaries, and many studies indicate these hospitals are absolutely correct that the DRG payment does not adequately compensate for the actual cost of care delivered. For a while, hospitals simply increased the charges for the same kinds of care to private insurance payers for non-Medicare beneficiaries. This cost-shifting worked for a while, but then the private payers fought back and limited what they would pay hospitals for those procedures.

What is lost in most of the debates about this radical change in payments for health care services for

Medicare beneficiaries is that for the first time the federal government shifted the emphasis of the program from a health care provider that provided needed medical care to its beneficiaries to a budget-driven payment system that looked to procedures that needed to be used to cut payment levels to match revenues. While needed, it signaled a fundamental philosophical shift that has never really swung back to emphasis on patient care.

In the early 1980s, the Health Care Finance Administration (HCFA), which is the government agency that runs Medicare, as a matter of practice determined which medical procedures would be reimbursed for Medicare beneficiaries. Private insurers would typically follow HCFA's lead on reimbursement for new medical procedures that transitioned from experimental procedures to those proven valuable in reducing morbidity or extending a patient's life. During that period HCFA refused to recognize heart transplants as a safe and effective procedure despite clear medical evidence that this procedure was safe, it could be performed with a high degree of reliability, and it saved lives.

Heart transplants were too expensive, and adding them to approved procedures was not something over which HCFA wanted to incur the wrath of the Office of Management and Budget (OMB). In fact, OMB directed that heart transplants remain as an experimental procedure long after it should have been approved for reimbursement.

That is an ugly secret the government would just as soon you didn't know anything about.

Americans have long touted our medical care delivery system as the very best in the world, and it is. Lack of finances and capable providers have resulted in the widespread rationing within Britain's socialized health care system that has drawn much criticism from across the Atlantic. But the U.S. government-imposed rationing, similar to the United Kingdom's, threatens top-notch quality in health care. Socialized medicine is a tragedy wherever employed.

American health care public policy makers did not want to acknowledge that we had reached a point where "rationing" of heart transplants was a part of our health care delivery system. Calling this procedure "experimental" allowed for some face-saving by HCFA bureaucrats, but it simply forestalled the day of reckoning when we would have to implement rationing procedures.

Today, beyond the natural rationing that occurs with the limited supply of transplantable hearts, Medicare also has a policy of limiting transplants to certain patient profiles; this ensures that if you are older and sicker you will be behind younger and healthier transplant candidates. That translates to the harsh reality that in America today if you are older and sicker, you are not going to receive a needed heart transplant. It is a natural consequence of a system that bases its thinking on the financial bottom line rather than on legitimate need for medical services.

That economic rationing is now extending itself into more basic Medicare benefits. Medicare was originally conceived as a program to provide insurance coverage similar in structure and scope to that enjoyed by those still working and their families. Over the past two decades however, escalating Medicare costs have forced a variety of benefit reductions or outright elimination of previously covered procedures. Today, working families generally enjoy a much broader health care coverage program than enjoyed by Medicare beneficiaries, and that gap is going to widen dramatically if Congress stays on its present philosophical course with regard to Medicare.

There are some things that can and should be done to shore up the Medicare system. First, there should be consideration for those current beneficiaries who looked at the Medicare program they were investing in and made specific decisions in their retirement planning based upon what they thought they were going to receive under Medicare. In legal parlance, that is a contract. But the Congress breaches that contract by continually eroding promised benefits.

An individual retiring today is unfairly penalized because the benefit package they were told would be available when they were planning for their retirement not only has fewer benefits, but it costs a whole lot more too. Congress should protect these workers and lock in their benefits within a reasonable time prior to retirement to allow them to plan for what funds they will need to protect their health care benefits.

Medicare beneficiaries deserve the opportunity to have choices in how they want to access the medical care delivery system. Whether the choice is keeping a fee-for-service doctor or joining some managed care program, the right to choose should be preserved. Those choices are currently on the brink of elimination with many of the proposals Congress is now contemplating.

A change in the Medicare reimbursement law contained a provision in the 1997 Balanced Budget Act (BBA), effective January 1, 1998, that essentially states that if a Medicare beneficiary wants to privately contract with his or her physician for a medical service that might otherwise be covered by Medicare Part B, then that physician must agree not to participate in Medicare for a period of no less than two years. Even Great Britain, the champion of socialized medicine, allows its seniors to pay privately for care outside of its restrictive system.

This issue arose from a 1992 lawsuit filed by several Medicare beneficiaries against HCFA and the then-Secretary of Health and Human Services, Louis Sullivan. HCFA had been threatening doctors for years with severe penalties if they privately contracted with patients. One patient involved in the suit had been told by HCFA that he could not personally pay for a service he wanted because HCFA had determined that it was not medically necessary. This patient wanted medical care, and was willing to pay for it personally. A fellow plaintiff had equally compelling complaints: his doctor wanted to waive the deductible for a covered Medicare procedure, and was willing to waive all of the Medicare portion of the payment in an attempt to financially assist his patient. HCFA threatened to fine the doctor $2,000 if he performed the procedure without billing Medicare and collecting a deductible from the patient.

A federal judge, in a rare and uncharacteristic bit of wisdom, ruled that HCFA had no right to prohibit such private contracting. But HCFA, undeterred in its zeal to continue harassing doctors, issued warning letters to physicians that if they accepted a private contract they would be penalized. Congress included language allowing such private contracting in the original version of BBA, but had to yield on the point in the face of a Clinton veto and was forced to pass a provision that allowed for private contracting but prohibited the contracted provider participation in Medicare for two years.

Senator Jon Kyl (R-Arizona) has filed legislation to correct this problem, and has persuaded HCFA to back off its previous threats for the time being to penalize doctors for contracting privately with Medicare patients. Senator Kyl's legislation allows seniors the opportunity to choose to pay personally for any desired health care service, whether it is covered by Medicare or not, and to purchase that service from any doctor or health care provider they choose.

Lined up in opposition is Congressman Fortney "Pete" Stark (D-California), joined by AARP, in open defiance of reason and freedom of choice for seniors. Congressman Stark has been a vocal proponent of a single-payer, government run, national health insurance program. He is committed to socialized medicine in America, and the private contracting issue runs counter to his view of socialized medicine. AARP's opposition on private contracting is one of a long line of issues where AARP sides with the big government bureaucrats in opposition to the rights of seniors.

The private contracting issue is only one example of Medicare's need for realignment. The BBA did include a provision for seniors to access a dramatic new and innovative financing mechanism for health care services called Medical Savings Accounts (MSAs). MSAs allow a Medicare beneficiary to put the difference between the costs of a contracted medical plan and what Medicare normally pays into a Medical Savings Account controlled by the beneficiary. Unfortunately, Congress limited this program to just 390,000 enrollees over a five-year test period and HCFA has been so negative about this service delivery option that it does not appear that MSAs will get much of a fair evaluation. It is, nonetheless, a very good program that could provide beneficiaries with an excellent choice for medical care.

One of the most encouraging new programs adopted by Congress is a demonstration project for

Medicare beneficiaries based on the Federal Employees Health Benefits Program (FEHBP). Senators John Breaux (D-Louisiana) and Connie Mack (R-Florida) have joined forces to promote a test where seniors can essentially receive the same care that a Member of Congress presently enjoys. This is the model for future solvency in the Medicare system when the baby boomers hit Medicare age.

The concept is a relatively simple one: give beneficiaries the power to contract with whatever provider plan they choose. Providers must meet certain minimum solvency requirements and consumer protection standards; after that, it is a question of competition in the market place so that a wide variety of choices are available to beneficiaries. Choice and competition are the keys to a strong and effective economy and will be the keys to strong and effective health care for seniors.

Medicare must also throw out the current method of paying Medicare health maintenance organizations (HMOs) based upon the 95 percent of Medicare fee-for-service costs. This weakening, ill-conceived formula was cooked up in a late night negotiating session in 1983 and was not driven by any data to support the correct reimbursement level. There has been plenty of time to correct this formula, but no action has been taken in the 15 years since its enactment. The 95 percent reimbursement plan essentially overpays many HMOs, giving them the incentive to seek out only the healthiest enrollees. Ideally, HCFA should first solicit bids from private health plans to compete for seniors' health care dollars, and then refine the package of services through direct negotiations with the bidders. Then Medicare could agree to pay a portion of the premium up to a ceiling. This is not a new, radical idea; it is the system that the Federal Employees Health Benefit Program currently uses.

Seniors should then be free to switch health plans each year or return to the basic Medicare program in the same way that Federal employees have an "open season" on health care plan options each year. This freedom will provide incentives for competing health plans to offer the widest possible benefit package and allow seniors to shop for the best program for them.

Means testing of Medicare payments can be a viable option for future beneficiaries when they have the time to plan what contributions will be necessary to cover their health care needs. Applying a stringent means testing standard on present beneficiaries breaks the contract with seniors and unfairly penalizes those who have planned well for their retirement years. Current means testing proposals disproportionately punish seniors by effectively discriminating against those who have been the most prudent in their retirement planning. Phased in without onerous penalties for good financial decisions, means testing can be an acceptable program for baby boomers who have the time to prepare for such financial participation.

These recommendations form the basis for a

more rational and fair Medicare system for existing beneficiaries. What Medicare cannot be, now or in the future, is a vehicle for political chicanery such as that proposed by President Clinton in January 1998. Clinton wants to expand Medicare coverage to individuals as young as 55 years of age if they have been laid off or displaced from their jobs. This kind of political showmanship makes existing Medicare beneficiaries pawns in the cynical game of political-"chicken" that Clinton is playing with the Republican Congress. Clinton advisors argue privately that it is a no-lose proposition for Clinton. If the Republicans capitulate, which few observers expect, then Clinton will get the credit for expanding the program to what will be perceived as a needy segment of the population. If the Republicans throw out the proposal, Clinton gets all the political benefits of having fought the good fight for a group of unemployed and needy workers.

The real problem with all of this is Clinton's selection of Medicare as the stage for hyping his liberal philosophical bent for a national health care system. Senator Phil Gramm (R-Texas) said it right when he compared Clinton's new expansion of Medicare to "putting more people aboard the Titanic when the ship is sinking and there aren't even enough lifeboats for those presently on board."

Medicare is not welfare, and President Clinton should not try to convert it to or treat it like a welfare program. Medicare is an insurance program which is an earned right derived from the contributions every worker has put into it. Existing beneficiaries should have the same benefit package available to them that they expected when they were making those payments. Anything less is a fraud, and one of the most destructive ever perpetrated against America's seniors.

FRAUD #7:

THE KYOTO GLOBAL WARMING TREATY IS GOOD FOR AMERICANS

The United Nations "Global Climate Treaty" sounds, on the surface, like a terrific idea. Add to that the solid endorsement of President Bill Clinton and Vice President Al Gore, and this Treaty gives the appearance of being a compelling issue worthy of public support. But examination past the U.N. Climate Treaty polished outer package exposes serious problems within.

In short, this treaty is a fraud, and it is time we all knew precisely how a variety of world leaders are misleading their citizens. The treaty bases itself upon assumptions unacceptable to a great number of credible scientists.

The U.N. Climate Treaty stems from the claim that, due to man-made industries, the earth is heating up to potentially deadly levels that will essentially melt the polar ice cap and trigger an environmental disaster, wiping out the earth's population. The cataclysmic environmental episode will allegedly throw the globe into epidemics of disease and famine, coupled with an complete upheaval of weather patterns and seasonal changes.

These claims suffer from one defect. They are not even remotely grounded in any rational or responsible set of facts supporting such conclusions.

The truth: Since the U.S. government started measuring the Earth's temperatures in 1979, nearly two decades ago, the Earth is actually cooling by .037 degrees Celsius per decade. That translates to about 1/3 of a degree every ten years.

The truth: Naturally occurring water vapor makes up 98% of the so-called "greenhouse gases" that the environmentalists have named as the culprit in the global warming debate. Yet, the whole debate is centered on the human activities that impact the other 2% of these greenhouse gases.

The truth: Claims that global warming is increasing the severity of hurricanes is rebutted by Florida State University scientists who found that, in fact, hurricane severity is decreasing over time. These researchers have found that storms are no more severe in the 1990s than they were in the 1950s

Here's the real question. Why should we care if this treaty attempts to reduce greenhouse gas emissions, even if the pro-treaty scientists are wrong? We are told that it is an issue of clean air and clean water, and all of us support those goals.

The answer, however, boils down to one issue.

While the environmental extremists promote the arguably far-fetched theory that some sort of environmental apocalypse will occur without swift action, a verifiable economic disaster looms for every American family if or when this treaty is ratified by the United States Senate and subsequently adopted by other global leaders.

Simply put, the so-called Kyoto Treaty will take money out of the pockets of every American family, particularly impacting senior citizens on fixed incomes and low-income families, thereby reducing the amount of money they have available for food, clothing, shelter, medical expenses, education, savings, and other important economic priorities they have for themselves and their families.

The treaty document, approved by the United Nations sponsored meeting in Kyoto, Japan in December 1997, has established a set of firm targets and timetables for restricting emissions that will negatively impact every individual, family and community in the United States. U.S. Enforcement of the Kyoto Treaty's provisions will reduce the number of American jobs, sometimes radically, in every community, city, and state. It will also reduce the competitiveness of American businesses in global markets, thereby weakening America and its working families.

For their part, the Clinton-Gore Administration has worked hard to downplay the significance of the Kyoto Treaty's impact on American families and our economy. Since the signing of the treaty document in December 1997, Clinton and Gore have begun implementing its terms in an apparent effort to subvert the Constitutional requirement of the U.S. Senate to ratify this treaty.

The U.S. Senate's wariness toward ratification is real, and proponents of the Kyoto Treaty are literally scared to death that their "crown jewel" of radical global environmentalism may be defeated in the Senate. Prior to the Kyoto meeting, the U.S. Senate voted 95-0 to oppose the treaty if it resulted in serious economic harm to the United States or if it failed to include the "developing countries" that its planners had specifically excluded from having to agree to the same limits as the United States, Australia, and the other nations in the category characterized as "Annex I" countries.

This resolution, dubbed the Byrd-Hagel resolution, named for the two Senators who sponsored the resolution — Senators Robert Byrd (D-West Virginia) and Chuck Hagel (R-Nebraska) — sent a clear unmistakable signal to the Clinton Administration on what the U.S. Senate would not accept from the negotiations at the Kyoto meeting. Instead of working to modify the provisions of the Treaty to comply with the Byrd-Hagel resolution, the Clinton Administration has engaged in a deliberate attempt to mislead and distort the actual language of the Treaty to their political advantage.

Clinton's Undersecretary of State, Timothy Wirth, who personally played a major role in negotiations on the Treaty, laid the foundation in

1988 for the Clinton philosophy on the international treaty that prevails today:

> *"We've got to ride the global warming issue. Even if the theory . . . is wrong, we will be doing the right thing, in terms of economic . . . and environmental policy."*

A United Nations scientific report on the greenhouse gas theory was altered by U.N. policymakers to remove the scientists' caveats, such as "None of the studies cited above has shown clear evidence that we can attribute the observed changes to the specific cause of increases in greenhouse gases."

The Department of Energy (DOE) has undertaken a major economic impact study which was completed in February 1997, but has since been withheld by Clinton Administration political employees because it undermines the Clinton-Gore argument supporting the Treaty. That DOE study concluded, for example, that the Treaty would "devastate the US steel industry," causing 80,000 lost steelworker jobs.

That's 80,000 steelworker families thrown out of work and into economic devastation merely to promote a false political agenda of Al Gore and President Clinton. It seems an unfairly large sacrifice to be forced out of American working families just to add a cheap political bullet point to Al Gore's Presidential campaign literature for the 2000 election year.

The Kyoto Treaty isn't the only environmental

smoke-and-mirrors charade the Clinton Administration has pulled on the American public. A report published by the National Center for Policy Analysis in July 1997 exposed another serious breach of trust between President Clinton and the American workforce.

The Environmental Protection Agency (EPA) promulgated stringent clean air regulations in November 1996 ostensibly to save the lives of asthmatic children. At the behest of a bipartisan group of the nation's mayors and governors, some Congressional Democrats led the fight to stop implementation of the standards until more evidence is compiled on the health effects of soot and smog.

In this case, the levels of these pollutants have declined substantially over the past 25 years. The EPA credits the Congressional clean air laws, but the fact is the levels of these pollutants actually fell more rapidly throughout the 1960s, prior to passage of the first Clean Air Act by the U.S. Congress.

But here is one of the Clinton EPA's dirty little secrets. The asthma rates which would supposedly be improved with the implementation of these regulations won't affect asthma deaths in children at all. While asthma rates in the United States have been climbing, the ground-level ozone rates have fallen dramatically over the past 20 years.

♦ Scientific data shows that levels of ozone decreased by 18.5 percent since 1974.

- ♦ Asthma rates have been increasing in all industrialized nations, rising by 45 percent in the United States in the last decade alone.

- ♦ Comprehensive studies by the European Federation of Asthma and Allergy Associations found that sedentary lifestyles in Western developed countries and indoor air problems are the primary causes of the recent increase in asthma.

- ♦ A July 1996 study by the National Institute of Allergy and Infectious Diseases concluded that by far the leading cause of asthma is an allergic reaction to cockroach droppings and carcasses.

- ♦ The EPA's own members of the Clean Air Scientific Advisory Committee do not agree with EPA Administrator Carol Browner that the science supporting the EPA regulations was indisputable:

  - Eight committee members thought no standards are justified because there is no clear evidence that setting a standard would yield tangible health benefits.

  - The remaining 13 members of the panel were split over whether current standards are too strict, not strict enough, or just about right.

Is it any wonder we lose confidence on our elected leaders?

But, sadly, there's more.

The Kyoto Treaty, and the rhetoric generated by those who support its ratification, is full of the same kinds of lies, distortions and half-truths that riddle the asthma issue with the EPA.

U.S. Senator Mike Enzi of Wyoming made the long trip to Japan to personally observe the negotiations in early December 1997 to determine for himself what the truth is. His assessment, after closely monitoring the negotiations, was damning. Senator Enzi called the Kyoto negotiations a "Chinese plot to restrict the growth of the American economy."

Senator Enzi pointed to the flat refusal by the People's Republic of China to join the UN's incipient global energy rationing regime.

Senator Chuck Hagel of Nebraska went to Kyoto, too, and he observed actions which led to the conclusion that the negotiators were ignoring the formidable scientific evidence which questioned the global warming hypothesis and felt those negotiators were doing their best to suppress open and honest scientific debate on this issue.

There was one humorous event from Kyoto that illustrates how creative the environmental extremists are in misleading the public. The environmentalists arranged for three ice sculptures, in the shape of penguins, to be placed just outside the Kyoto conference hall where the negotiations were taking place. They anticipated a quick "meltdown" of the penguin ice sculptures. Their point was to show that "global warming" was melting the environment.

Unfortunately, Mother Nature wasn't cooperating with their contrived political stunt. It was so cold in Kyoto that conference negotiators were even walking around indoors with coats, scarves, and even gloves. The ice sculpture penguins lasted through the conference.

But the lesson behind all of that is the sad fact that many Americans may end up in the same position having to wear coats, scarves, and gloves indoors because the price of energy to heat their homes is now unaffordable. Or, in the suffocating heat of summer, Americans will suffer the effects of potentially deadly hot temperatures because they cannot afford to cool their homes. These are the plausible results of environmental fanaticism over an issue that lacks a scientific basis for action.

Americans should not be lulled into a false sense of confidence from that 95-0 vote in the Byrd-Hagel resolution. Even if the U.S. Senate were inclined to reject the Kyoto Treaty today, the Clinton Administration has refused to submit it for ratification. And they do not plan to do so anytime in the near future, possibly not until mid-1999.

In the interim, Bill Clinton and Al Gore have an alternate strategy for implementing their extremist environmental agenda. This backdoor imple-mentation of the Kyoto Treaty is wrong, and arguably unconstitutional. Unfortunately, this deliberate subterfuge may slip under the radar screen of the national media and the Congress.

For public assuagement, the Clinton

Administration routinely issues its denials about backdoor implementation of the Kyoto Treaty. Undersecretary of State Stuart Eizenstat told the Senate Foreign Relations Committee: "We have no intention, through the backdoor or anything else, of trying to impose or take any steps to impose what would be binding restrictions on our companies, on our industry, on our business, or on our agriculture, or on our commerce, or on our country until and unless the Senate of the United States says so."

While Undersecretary Eizenstat was saying what needed to be said to the U.S. Senate, the EPA has nonetheless developed a legal theory claiming its own necessary authority under the existing Clean Air Act to restrict carbon dioxide emissions without Congressional approval. This EPA document argues that it does not need Senate ratification to implement the greenhouse gas emissions budget required under the Kyoto protocol.

The Clinton Administration trotted down this deceptive path in Japan, attempting implementation of the same standards by using a questionable claim of regulatory authority. EPA Administrator Browning testified before the House VA, HUD, and Independent Agencies Appropriations Committee about a newly-conceived Administrative initiative called "The Climate Change Technology Initiative" which involves EPA, DOE, and HUD. Administrator Browning claimed that EPA's share of $205 million " will help America meet its global new [sic] responsibility to reduce greenhouse gas emissions through market forces, new technology, and energy efficiency."

That's fraud, and they know it.

Here's what those new responsibilities will cost individual American families.

The U.S. agreed to reduce its emissions to 7 percent below 1990 levels by 2008-2012, amounting to a 40% reduction of predicted emission levels by the year 2010.

In California alone, such a drastic reduction equates to a loss of 300,000 jobs and will force wages to fall by as much as 3.2 percent. The economic impact study documenting this upheaval, conducted by the non-partisan Wharton Econometrics Forecasting Associates, concludes that residential electricity rates would increase by 29 percent, home heating oil by 53 percent, and natural gas by 52 percent.

But California would not be the only state to suffer. The Kyoto Treaty would put 110,000 New Yorkers and 123,000 Texans out of work. Job-losses and utility price-hike problems would hit hard across America. If Kyoto wins, America will lose.

Other studies conclude that gasoline prices at the pump could increase by 50 cents a gallon, effectively locking many American seniors in their homes because they can no longer afford to buy fuel for their automobiles.

But those homes will not be as comfortable, thanks to treaty-borne jumps in cooling and heating costs that will prove too great a strain on families and seniors on fixed incomes. Consequently, the absence of temperature control in homes could threaten good health and create possible death traps for fragile seniors.

President Clinton's band of radical global warming advocates attempt to offset the adverse health impacts of the Treaty on seniors by claiming that unproven global warming will result in a scary epidemic of malaria, dengue, and yellow fever. Those claims simply do not stand up to any reasonable scrutiny.

In a letter published by Dr. Paul Reitner of the Center for Disease Control and Prevention in the March 14, 1998 issue of *Lancet* writes that "malaria was a common disease throughout much of the USA, and it remained endemic until the 1950s." Yellow and dengue fever were also common until the 1940s. Reitner observed that "Even in the present century, devastating epidemics [of malaria] occurred as far north as Archangel on the Arctic Circle, and disease remained endemic in such untropical countries as Holland, Poland, and Finland until after World War II." The truth is that such outbreaks of malaria and other related diseases are related to factors which have nothing to do with climate and a lot to do with public health practices used to control such diseases.

Interestingly, if global warming did occur, the world population would in many ways benefit. For example, the World Bank estimates that fully one-third of the world's population already suffers from chronic water shortages. The Worldwatch Institute predicts that this situation will be exacerbated further by the addition of an estimated 2.6 billion people to the world's population over the next 30 years. By 2025, the group claims some 3 billion people, over 40% of the world's population, could be living in countries without sufficient water supplies. That would lead to crop failures, diminished economic development and even to regional conflicts as nations find it necessary to fight for control over scarce water resources.

Global warming would mean more condensation and more evaporation, producing more and perhaps even heavier rains. Global warming could, therefore, offer the answer to the water scarcity problem that the environmentalists have been seeking.

It is interesting to note that 1998 marked the year of El Nino, which accounted for a disruptive and turbulent year of uncommon weather patterns. This naturally occurring phenomenon has nothing to do with global warming, but it has had a far more powerful effect on us than global warming.

No matter which side of the scientific haggling ends up winning the intellectual wars, there is one incredibly important argument that will compel the U.S. Senate to reject this treaty: it is not fair.

There are 134 of 173 countries who are exempt from the emission limitations of the Treaty. And the ones who are exempt include some of the fastest developing nations, like South Korea, India, Mexico and China. It means that there will be a dramatic shift in economic growth, but no reduction in greenhouse gases.

Essentially, American jobs will be shifted overseas, and none of the environmental goals of the Kyoto Treaty will be met.

Nona Wegner, Vice President of The Seniors Coalition, was quoted in national news interviews saying that "skyrocketing fuel costs are the worst nightmare of every senior citizen who lives on a fixed income and marshals their resources to take care of themselves and have a little left over to visit their families. It is a knife that cuts past the quick and into their very hearts."

The assessment of Stephen L. Miller, President of the Center for Energy and Economic Development, puts the issue in proper perspective:

> *"The proposed Kyoto Treaty is like a card game where the deck is stacked. American workers are being dealt a losing hand through the negotiating process. In the end, there will be no real environmental benefit and America's working families will be forced to pay higher energy and consumer costs while we export U.S. jobs to countries that are exempted from action under the treaty."*

Every one of us has picked up the telephone and heard the sweet voice on the other end politely inquiring if you have a moment to answer just a few questions about our quality of life. As good citizens, and if the timing is convenient, we all are generally happy to participate in what has become an important part of American democracy. Public opinion polls today are used extensively by opinion leaders and elected officials to test the public's viewpoint.

I recently answered such a phone call and was asked if I supported efforts to make sure we have clean water to drink every day. The question, I must admit, set me back a little. I quickly asked myself what kind of person would answer that question with anything but a "yes." That was the answer I offered to the pollster, and I felt proud to do so.

The next question queried whether I supported efforts to make sure we have clean air to breathe. In the back of my mind, I pegged this poll as one sponsored by some radical environmental group, and I looked for some way to hedge my answer.

I told the pollster that I supported "reasonable efforts" to clean up the air.

"Then I can mark your answer as a 'yes' to that question?"

Now I was trapped. If I said no, then I was placed in the uncomfortable position of being cast as a supporter of the corporate polluters who place profits over the public health. If I said yes, I figured that my answer was going to be a part of some extensive lobbying effort to convince the U.S. Congress to shut down every manufacturing operation in America.

I meekly assented that my answer was "yes." I suddenly felt nervous, and wondered silently how such a phone call could put me in such a vulnerable position.

Then, the pollster inquired if I supported efforts to help developing nations to improve economic opportunities for otherwise impoverished citizens. The images of poverty and suffering in third world countries have flashed across television news programs and public service announcements for years. Who doesn't support efforts for developing nations to improve economic opportunities that will allow families to improve the quality of their lives?

Now, I'm not just nervous, I'm panicked.

I conjured up the thought that some anonymous extremist environmental activist was already plotting how to label my answers as part of that vast silent majority known euphemistically as "middle America" was now supporting tough new environmental restrictions. I was right to have reservations about how my answers were going to be used, but I didn't really know just how right I was.

The radical environmentalist movement in America wants to shut down the industrialized economies of developed nations to fit their narrow, often bizarre extremist agenda. The effect of this extremism would spell economic disaster for working families and a trip down the slippery slope of Americans subsidizing the economic development of third world countries. It would not be a pleasant journey, because to meet the goals set by these global environmental extremists, it would unfairly rob America of its financial strength and sap the incentives for improving the quality of lives for our families.

For me, that's not just unfair, it's a flat out fraud.

FRAUD #8:

YOUR CONGRESSMAN REPRESENTS YOU IN CONGRESS

One of the great frauds in American politics is the notion that your Congressman and Senators represent you, your neighbors, and those residing within the boundaries of the congressional district or state in which you live. You may think your Congressman should represent your interests, and it may well have been precisely what the founders of our country anticipated when they drafted the Constitution. But it is not the way politics works today.

Two dangerous elements in the political system deter and debilitate the kind of representative democracy our Founding Fathers envisioned: money and power. Money is the lubricant that too often determines who gains access to a Congressman or Senator on all-important votes. Power in politics comes from a combination of seniority and committee assignments acquired over the years.

Money and power together breed corruption and feed fraud.

The money part of the equation is difficult to control. As long as we subscribe to a system of campaign financing that affords individual citizens the right to contribute to candidates of their choice, anyone, including those who differ dramatically on the issues of concern to you, will maintain the freedom to make those contributions. Abuses of financial contributions and political perks makes a mockery of campaign finance freedoms and our representative democracy.

Money-derived corruption within the political system is clearly evident. High-profile showcases of greed include the likes of Congressman Dan Rostenkowski (D-Illinois) who, for instance, converted taxpayer-funded and campaign-purchased postage stamps for cash. Dan Rostenkowski was, at the time of the charges, arguably one of the most powerful and prominent men in America serving as the Chairman of the House Ways and Means Committee, which establishes tax policy and governs much of the financial systems in America. The specter of Chairman Rostenkowski hustling down to the House Post Office to turn in stamps which should have been used for mail going out of his office simply to collect a little pocket change illustrates perfectly the depth of abuse of trust in politics.

In his book, *Ethics in Congress: From Individual to Institutional Corruption,* Harvard political scientist Dennis Thompson makes the interesting observation that more Members of Congress have been investigated and sanctioned for misconduct in the past decade and a half than in the entire previous history of the Congress. "But," Thompson maintains, "individual members are probably less corrupt than they used to be. Conduct generally accepted in earlier eras may now be grounds for expulsion."

It may be reassuring that we are raising the bar for improved standards of conduct, but the cases of corruption are nonetheless important warning signals for how our Members of Congress are so easily diverted in their interest for personal gain from the legitimate interests of their constituents. A classic example is the "Keating Five" scandal which involved a group of prominent Senators who were accused of improperly intervening in the government's regulation of a financial institution owned by a major campaign contributor. Charles Keating, the major contributor, and his lobbyists had "bought" virtually full access to each of these Senators, a privilege not readily available to most constituents, even those who make reasonable and typical campaign contributions.

The book deals of former Senator David Durenberger and House Speaker Jim Wright; the indiscretion of Senator D'Amato allowing his brother to use his Senate office to conduct a lobbying business; the ABSCAM case in the 1980s in which six House Members and one Senator were convicted of helping FBI agents disguised as Arab sheiks obtain approval to emigrate to the United States in return for cash and gifts; all combine to erode the public confidence in our elected officials.

The saddest commentary about the abuses attributable to the negative influence of money in the political system comes through in Senator Alan Cranston's personal defense for his involvement in the Keating Five scandal: "Everybody is doing it."

The appeal of seniority in the Congress can also lure a Congressman or Senator away from his or her responsibilities to those at home. When a Congressman is assigned to a Committee, even if it is important to his or her home district, its range of issues covered is typically of major interest to a much narrower corporate constituency. The more seniority the Representative has, the less he or she is apt to represent the individual interests of his or her home district constituents. The committee system in the Congress is the source of power for Members of Congress, and they use their committee position to further a wide range of campaign and political interests.

If you are lucky enough to live in some area where the committee assignment of your Representative meshes with the interests of his or her constituents, then you may be fortunate enough to receive a "bonus representation." But "bonus representation" applies only if the lobbying interests working that committee also support the position you want your Congressman to take on a given issue. If the issues conflict, your Congressman will often sacrifice support for his home district. That will no doubt be followed by a lot of political doublespeak to hide the true reason for the defection from constituent interest.

The more seniority a Member of Congress gets on committees, the less likely it is that he or she will side with the home district on critical issues. That is because the lobbyists keep steady pressure on your Congressman to favor their corporate interests. Those same lobbyists will be more than accommodating in coordinating some face-saving measures at home to cover that Congressman politically and to minimize any political damage.

It all sounds a bit bizarre, but it is precisely how the political game works in Washington.

There are actually two factors which influence committee assignments for Members of Congress that do not necessarily serve the interests of their constituents. First, when a Member is elected to their first term, he or she must generally take whatever committee slots that are available. Senators typically do not attain sufficient seniority to move to a committee of their choice until after four years in office; Congressmen usually wait two or three terms in office before finding a spot on their preferred committee. That certainly would account for some delay in a Member's ability to best serve the interests of his or her constituents. During that waiting period, the lobbyists on the committee to which that Member is assigned get their claws in deep, and the opportunity to switch requires the Member to forfeit the relationships they have built with industries and the lobbyists and campaign contributions that follow. Furthermore, a committee switch requires that the Member forfeit the expertise that comes with tenure on a committee. Most difficult for a Member is forfeiting seniority on the assigned committee to switch to another where his or her name goes to the bottom of the seniority list.

The second factor is more problematic for the constituents of a Member. Perhaps their Senator or Representative has no interest in the committee assignment or the issues on it, even though the committee may address issues that are critical to their home district. Whether it is the Member's professional background, educational focus, or personal interests which get in the way, the outcome is the same: the Member often follows personal interest if it overrides the constituent interest.

Whatever the reason, the reality in Washington is that power comes from seniority, and once a Member gets on a committee, it is unlikely he or she will shift unless it offers a particularly attractive political advantage to do so. Here is where seniors can make a big difference.

By working hard to weigh in with your Congressman, you can influence the decisions he or she may make on committee assignments that may be available from one Congress to the next. That means seniors will have to convince their Congressman or Senator that working to get on the committees that impact senior issues is a smart political move. If there is a void in the level of noise Congressmen or

Senators hear from home, you can be certain it will be filled by a willing lobbyist who wants their ear.

A good example of how Members may defer committee assignments even though they would be politically advantageous to their constituents involves Senator Orrin Hatch, who is referenced earlier in this book. Senator Hatch is now serving in his fourth term in the Senate. In the sixth year of his first term, Senator Hatch had the opportunity to sit on the Senate Energy and Natural Resources Committee. It was a plum assignment that any western Senator would love to have. The problem: Senator Hatch wanted to go to the Senate Judiciary Committee, and did not want to jump from his Labor Committee slot because he had high seniority there. Since Hatch is an attorney by profession, and he loves the law first and foremost, he deferred taking the Energy and Natural Resources slot even though it may have been of enormous benefit to his state. Then, several years later, Hatch ascended to the Chairmanship of the Judiciary Committee, gave up his slot on the Labor Committee, and went to the Senate Finance Committee. In doing so, he passed up the plum Energy and Natural Resources slot again. This time he did so because he had become a champion of health care issues and the Senate Finance Committee offered the opportunity to seize the bully pulpit on health care financing issues.

The people of Utah have no representation on the Energy and Natural Resources Committee since their other Senator, Robert Bennett, sits on the

Appropriations, Banking, and Governmental Affairs Committee. For a state that was a leader in the "sagebrush rebellion," challenging federal ownership of more than 70 percent of Utah's land, it is a strange absence indeed. Hatch clinched the Chairmanship of a powerful Senate committee, but a committee whose constituency is the national legal community, not Utah.

West Virginia's Senator Robert Byrd sits on the Appropriations Committee, and he makes no bones about his perception of himself as a national leader in the U.S. Senate. The fact that he is from West Virginia is incidental. It is ironic that a man who perceives himself to be a uniquely national leader happens to be in a position to send billions in pork to his home state, which he does to keep his constituents too busy spending all that federal money to worry that there might be better committee alignments more suited to the concerns of West Virginians for Senator Byrd.

It may seem that I am picking on Senator Hatch a little, but I have only offered some examples here to illustrate what happens to a Senator or Congressman when they hit Washington, D.C. I remember how stunned I was when I heard that Orrin Hatch had joined forces with the likes of Senator Ted Kennedy to sponsor a bill that is known as the "Kiddiecare" insurance bill. That legislation is an integral part of the liberal, big-government health care plan that Clinton wants to incrementally pass as part of his socialized medicine health care scheme. I can tell you that Senator Hatch, when he is at home in Utah, has to talk fast to hoodwink his constituents on that issue. The point is, Senator Hatch may not be any better or worse than your own Senator or Congressman. Many of them say one thing at home, but in Washington they act far differently. You need to look hard at your own Congressional delegation to see if the same kinds of problems exist there. If you look closely enough, I'll bet you see the very same kind of behavior out of many in the Congress.

The point is, sending someone to Congress does not mean they will automatically represent the interests of their district. Some will, however, especially in cases where constituents express their needs and pressure legislators to respond. After all, these officials do want to get reelected, so they at least to some degree have to listen to the home folks.

Most important, the people who have the ear of your Congressman or Senator are those who bang on their door day after day. These are the paid lobbyists who make it their business to capture the ear and heart of your Congressman or Senator, even if their interests are opposed to yours.

The key to breaking this money/power lock on your Congressman is actually quite simple to achieve. The source of the power is the office those Congressman and Senators hold. The keys to that power, and the access to that money, is held by the voters at home. The problem is that too few of these voters tell their Congressmen or Senators that they want them to be accountable. That accountability can be force-fed to your Senator, but it requires some action.

Seniors are the most powerful voting bloc in the electorate. That is muscle that has to be flexed, and it begins with you. The "Solutions" chapter at the end of this book shows you how to assert your strength and demand accountability from our legislators. Taken seriously, seniors can help to clean up the corruption and help their Congressmen and Senators focus on issues that are of real importance to constituents.

FRAUD #9:

ELECTRICITY DEREGULATION WOULD BE BAD FOR ALL CONSUMERS, INCLUDING SENIORS

In our topsy-turvy world, there are some things that are absolutes, such as the monthly process of paying our utility bills. It's not something we think much about at all; we just pay the amount and shrug our shoulders. And we know that when we turn on the lights, or watch television, or just read a good book by the light of the lamp by our bed, that the electricity is there and there isn't one thing we could do to change anything about how that electricity gets to that light or how much it will cost us.

This portrait of consumer submission and indifference is completely false and distorted, but it is how a lot of executives in the electric generation companies like to think of us and they treat us accordingly. It is a fraud, and we can do something to expose and correct it.

Electrical generating capacity is going through exactly the same market upheaval experienced in the telephone industry just over a decade ago. Even though the subject seems a little mundane, it actually is a hot topic among state and federal elected officials and the bureaucrats who staff our regulatory agencies. The cost of electricity is about to go competitive.

Some of the fears are the same ones we worried about with telephones. If we have more than one telephone company, are we going to have multiple sets of phone lines crisscrossing our neighborhoods for every company that jumps into the business? And how can any one company afford the investment in the infrastructure of those telephone lines and be price competitive with the original telephone company?

What happens in the electrical industry deregulation debate will have dramatic implications for natural gas, telecommunications, airlines, trucking and railroads. Those utilities presently have enormous economic impacts on every aspect of our lives, and every one of us has a major stake in how public policy is formulated in this area.

With the electric industry, the most far-reaching proposal under consideration is that every consumer would have a choice in who their electricity supplier is going to be. Electric utilities will lose their monopoly rights to sell to specific sets of customers. These utilities would be converted to transporters of electricity (eliminating the multiple lines problems) but the generation of the electricity and the end user delivery would be opened up to free-market competition. Under this plan, the only segment of the electric industry that would be regulated would be the transport of that electricity.

As radical as it sounds, this same kind of progressive transition to competition has already occurred in several industries that operate under the same economic and distribution model as electricity. These industries are commonly referred to as "network" industries since the suppliers and customers are connected by a network of rails, pipes, wire lines, roads or air routes. In these kinds of distribution systems, the decision of one part of the network directly impacts each of the other parts of the network.

The bottom line is astounding. American residential consumers lay out $90 billion annually to keep those lights on, heating their homes and water, and to power up their computers and other electrical appliances. Our industrial plants run up electric bills of $47 billion a year, and the service sector chalks up an additional $68 billion every year. In total, this is a huge issue that has far-reaching economic consequences for every consumer.

Deregulation of the electrical industry so that the 3,200 electric utilities in America would actually have to compete with one another offers a real promise of dramatic savings for consumers. Furthermore, we would see measurable increase in the quality and range of services that would be available to consumers and other electrical customers. In a study by the Brookings Institution in 1997, five industries that had undergone the transition from a totally regulated network to some form of open competition had prices paid by consumers fall significantly as a result of the deregulation. Within the first two years of deregulation, prices fell by 4 to 15 percent and sometimes more for certain segments of customers. Within 10 years, prices were at least 25 percent lower, sometimes 50 percent lower. While not all of these pricing changes can be traced directly to deregulation, study after study has demonstrated that regulatory reforms have created billion of dollars worth of consumer benefits.

Advocates of this deregulation contend there will be three significant advantages for consumers if the Congress has the political will to enact a responsible deregulation plan.

♦ **Consumers will save as much as 42% on electric bills.** Just the prospect of those kinds of savings are enough to open the eyes of even the most cynical opponents of electric deregulation. Those states where partial deregulation has already occurred and customers have the right to choose a provider have seen rates go down by 10 to 20 percent. Full deregulation will make the target of 40 percent savings or more well within reach. The savings on residential electricity bills will not be the only bottom-line economic impact. Every industry and service in America which uses electricity in their business will see reductions in costs for the production and marketing of their goods and services. The ripple effect will manifest itself in the marketplace with reduced prices for a wide range of goods and services. A National Taxpayers Union study found that competition in the electric industry will slash the federal deficit by $67 billion over five years. Local government will also benefit as schools, hospitals, and libraries spend less on electricity.

♦ **Competition will expand choices and services.** Every one of us knows what it's like to look at the electric meter. It might as well be an Egyptian hieroglyphic because it is nearly impossible for consumers to read. With competition, our meters will be easy to read and allow customers to actually reduce energy consumption when the rates are the highest and increase it when the rates are lower. Most important, consumers will have the choice. We will also see new billing payment options that will include such services as fixed monthly billing that can be incorporated in your mortgage or rent to simplify bill paying.

♦ **Improved reliability and enhanced environmental features.** Competition is about winning customers, and it thus forces providers to improve the reliability of their systems to win and keep those customers. Consumers who don't like the level of service, when they have a choice, can switch to another provider. When competition is open, electric generation options that are friendlier to the environment will become viable choices. Renewable energy sources such as wind turbines and solar cells will be a part of the competitive marketplace.

The bottom line for consumers is that open competition could end up producing as much as $300 in savings every month in disposable income that is churning in the regulated system right now. That is money that is going to corporate giant electrical monopolies rather than in consumers' pockets. In a deregulated system consumers really can make intelligent choices that will favorably impact their bottom line.

If you want an example you can really get your arms around where deregulation of a public monopoly actually worked, you don't have to look much further than the airline industry.

When deregulation of airlines hit, price competition for non-business travelers led to an explosion in air travel. Consumers who never thought they would see the inside of an airliner, let alone fly on one, suddenly found the low fares that empowered them to travel to Yellowstone, Hawaii, or Florida for family vacations. They could suddenly afford a service that had been beyond their economic reach while it was a regulated monopoly. Service in the airline industry improved dramatically along with the rapid expansion in passenger miles flown.

The airline deregulation plan was followed by

similar deregulation of natural gas production and long-distance telecommunication. The result was predictable and consistent: lower prices and expanded quality of services. Market deregulation works, and its track record gives public policy makers deep confidence that electrical deregulation will work too.

The major stumbling block to these reforms is the existing dinosaur electrical monopolies. With as much money that is in the system now, the money for Washington lobbyists and gushing political action committee funds have set the stage for diverting Congress from what should be a clear decision. This infusion of lobbying capital has energized key lobbyists with a single goal of creating confusion about what legislative initiative is the most appropriate one to apply to deregulation of the electrical industry.

The buzzword in the electrical industry has always been "economies of scale." The theory was that in order to build the capital to construct a nationwide distribution system, a public monopoly had to be granted to some electrical provider. These monopolies were divvied up between various geographical centers to service consumers. In exchange for the monopoly, these companies submitted themselves to rate controls that were supposed to protect consumers from exploitative pricing. But consumers receive no protection.

Supporters of these public monopolies point out that the system delivers a reliable source of power to a growing nation and this monopoly has been able to provide this product with rate increases that are typically less than the annual consumer price index. But even the most ardent supporters of regulated utilities acknowledge that the system needs to be changed because the public monopoly has been a breeding ground for waste, inefficiency, and high rates to consumers.

If nothing else, new technology demands changes in the regulated utilities, but there has been little impetus until the threat of deregulation now has them issuing a flood of promises for internal reforms. A couple of significant technology advances, coupled with price reduction in natural gas, have dramatically changed the equation in electricity generation. For example, this new technology has resulted in small generating stations that in many cases were just as efficient, if not more so, than the huge coal and nuclear generating stations that have long provided the bulk of America's electrical energy.

The much touted "economies of scale" argument that justified making electricity generation a public monopoly has simply evaporated. The price for natural gas as the fuel for these small and efficient generating stations was the result of the deregulation of the natural gas network. Now, small entrepreneurs can and do build electricity generating plants that can offer reliable electricity generation to communities that previously had to buy from the huge monopoly giants.

Here's the most difficult problem if you are an advocate for public monopoly of the electrical generation network. These new start-up electrical generation companies can produce electricity and sell it on the open market at a profit for prices as low as one-half to one-third of the public utilities. The price reduction is possible because these electric utility monopolies are trapped in the capital recovery for the investment they made into nuclear power plants.

The argument divides essentially down two sides. On one hand, the utility companies argue they made the investments in expensive nuclear plants because of the requirement that they have the capacity to generate enough electricity so that on peak use days when every household turned on their air conditioners, there would be electricity to run them. When they failed, stories of "brown-outs" and power failures usually lead the local news. The telephone companies always knew that on peak use days like Mother's Day, there would be a percentage of calls that simply could not be accommodated on the network, and the system busy signal would create a minor inconvenience to customers.

Many of the stockholders in those electricity monopolies would also be negatively impacted if a public policy decision were made forcing utility companies to write off the investments in expensive nuclear plants and let the hit fall directly to the bottom line. Such a decision would make the stocks and bonds of these industries that many elderly have in their investment portfolios virtually worthless. Many legal scholars argue that such public policy decisions to switch from a regulated monopoly to market competition and force such write-offs would amount to an unconstitutional confiscation of the utilities' property.

Critics of the electric monopolies disagree, claiming that no justification exists for forcing consumers to bear the costs of mismanagement by these utilities. The only way that protection can be offered to the stockholders in such companies is to add a surcharge to the cost of electricity for every consumer. That, the critics contend, would be grossly unfair to consumers who would bear the brunt of the bad business decisions made by the managers of these utilities. It is not surprising that some of these decisions were made at a time when these managers thought that there was little or no risk in making such investments because the government would simply make consumers pay for pricey generation plants.

There are some formidable stumbling blocks in the path to deregulation of the electric industry. First, environmentalists have been reluctant to sign on, even though they literally hate the coal-fired and nuclear technology that has prevailed. Their ugly secret: the environmentalists fear losing the clout they have with the existing electrical monopolies. Fighting a market-based competitive industry would eliminate a hidden perk that environmentalists have long enjoyed. Environmentalists tied to the electricity monopolies have a full plate of pet projects for which they have been receiving funding from the electric utilities. These projects include costly conservation programs that have been hidden from consumers in the utility rates but that are the crown jewels of the environmentalists.

Another stumbling block stems from the fear held by a segment of the conservative community that deregulating the electric industry will strip states of the powers they currently hold. This objection contains a kernel of truth in that much of what is being done in individual states has been pushing the electric industry to more market-based competitive structures. Indeed, 13 states have already enacted some form of pro-competition regulatory reform, and 36 other states are in some stage of evaluating new reforms. The lone hold-out is South Dakota, which seems stuck in the rut of total monopolistic control. The problem for states' rights advocates, however, is that the jurisdiction over interstate electric transmission lines is solely an issue for federal regulators, and access to these lines is the key to success of market-based competition.

One of the possible outcomes of this debate would not be good for consumers: a compromise where the deregulation would only apply to the wholesale electricity market. This situation would allow large customers to pick their suppliers, but would lock individual consumers out of the ability to choose between competitive providers. Limits on our choices cut short the cost savings and quality enhancements to service that we should be entitled to.

America needs to move forward now. California residents got the power to choose their electricity provider on January 1, 1998. There is absolutely no reason why every American cannot be similarly empowered to make that same choice in the next two years. Congress can establish broad guidelines and allow the states to work out the fine details of a deregulation plan, thus preserving the role of states in protecting their citizens. And the deregulation plan must reach consumers directly, allowing us to make our own decisions and to benefit from the market forces that will take over and drive better quality service in the future at more reasonable costs. Just as in the direct purchase of electricity for our homes, electricity deregulation will save the average American family $295 per year.

The time has come to shine a bright light on the electric utilities and their friends in the environmental community. It is a fraud that can and should be stopped with no further delay. This seemingly boring issue needs to be translated into an exciting and dynamic public policy change that will give consumers the choice they deserve in electricity use.

FRAUD #10:

EARNINGS LIMITS AND ESTATE TAXES ARE FAIR TAXES

Law enforcement officials warn anyone entering a crowded place to beware of pickpockets who can slyly steal a wallet without the victim's notice.

When it comes to such skilled sleight of hand, the U.S. Congress often has no peer among the common street thieves who prey on the unsuspecting. Its tools are benign sounding phrases like "earning limits" and "estate taxes." More than just words, they are descriptions of the legislative tools that Congress has enacted which have the same effect of taking taxpayers' hard-earned money from our pockets as any street pick-pocket artist.

Seniors are the only citizens in America whose income the government has the audacity to restrict. Characterized as tax policy and income adjustments, earnings limits and estate taxes are grand frauds upon America's seniors, and it is time they were exposed.

Earnings Limit

Let's first look at what earnings limits really are.

Simply put, the government has placed a limit on the amount of money that any social security recipient can earn without having some portion of their monthly benefit check forfeited to the government. Under current law, senior citizens between the ages of 65 and 69 lose one dollar in Social Security benefits for every three dollars they earn in 1998 above $23,000. That limit increases in 1999 to $27,000, and to $30,000 in the year 2000.

Congress passed the Social Security Act in 1935 during President Roosevelt's comprehensive "New Deal" legislative initiative. Among other things, the most important thing this legislation did for older Americans was establish a guaranteed income source for seniors who had retired.

It was a lesson learned from the Great Depression, and the inspiration for this Social Security program was derived sadly from the economic and psychological suffering that millions of seniors experienced when the American economy collapsed. At its core, the New Deal was supposed to preserve dignity for those who had worked their entire lives and who had expected to have a secure retirement.

At the outset, there was a provision in the Social Security Act which established an earnings limit. The rationale for this provision was rooted in the fact that the enactment of this Social Security system was initially funded for new benefit recipients from an unfunded Social Security Trust Fund.

That simply meant that the first social security beneficiaries were included in the system even though they had put funds into the Trust Fund for only a short period of time as opposed to the way that all present beneficiaries have participated over a much longer period. It would be very reasonable for an earnings limit to be imposed on those "unfunded" beneficiaries because only a portion of the benefits they were receiving at that time were funds they had contributed.

But once beneficiaries had fully funded themselves in the system by paying regular contributions to the Trust Fund during their working years, any justification to continue those earnings limits evaporates. What possible rationale could be used to penalize an active senior who chooses to work beyond normal retirement years?

Americans over the age of 65 currently number more than 30 million, accounting for 12 percent of the population. Our lifestyle choices are extending our life span, and facts show that today's Social Security beneficiaries are healthier and better able to be in the workplace than were their predecessors, and this trend will continue in the future.

Yet, despite these facts, the Congress has looked at earnings limits only as a source of income they can use to fund their own pet projects.

Attempts to correct this inequity and stop this fraud on seniors are often met with unfair accusations of greed. The truth is, it is the Congress that is guilty of greed. It is they who are picking the pockets of American seniors.

The fundamental problem is that the Congress views Social Security as a welfare program, not a retirement investment account. The money that they "dole" out to Social Security beneficiaries is our money, yet they treat it like it's tax revenue over which they have broad discretion.

At its inception, Social Security was supposed to compensate beneficiaries for lost income during retirement. The assumption was that seniors could obviously continue to work on their own and earn additional money. For those who chose to retire, the Social Security benefits were to be drawn from funds they contributed during all of their working lives.

If a worker entered the workforce at age 21 in the year of passage of the Social Security Act, when they turned 65 in 1979 they would have worked 44 years and contributed to the Trust Fund during their entire working lives. At a minimum, the earnings limits should not have applied to those "fully funded" beneficiaries.

Critics argue that present Social Security beneficiaries are taking more out of the Trust Funds than they invested in it. Strictly from an economic analysis, and without allowing for growth that would have occurred if the money had been invested prudently, that is true.

What is also true, and something critics willingly overlook, is that none of those beneficiaries had any say whatsoever in how the Social Security Trust Funds were invested to assure that the monies they had contributed were prudently invested to yield sufficient returns to outstrip inflation.

It is unfair to accuse innocent beneficiaries with drawing out more money than they put in when those beneficiaries could have taken that same money and invested it themselves and done much better than the government has in managing their retirement funds.

The earnings limits on social security beneficiaries should be repealed, and there is not one credible argument that can be advanced for its continued existence.

But the Congress is not presently inclined to do anything about this horrible fraud on America's senior citizens.

In fact, there is a strong pressure in the Congress to add even heavier burdens on older Americans and to resist any efforts to alleviate any of the unfair burdens heaped upon them.

A perfect example is the tax proposed by the Clinton Administration and passed by the Congress in 1993 that dramatically increased the amount of taxes that working seniors would have to pay on Social Security benefits if they had other income. The *1993 Omnibus Reconciliation Act (OBRA 1993)* set that threshold at $34,000 for seniors or $44,000 for couples which triggered a tax on 85 percent of Social Security benefits.

Intense pressure applied by The Seniors Coalition and other senior advocacy groups forced the Congress to pass the *Senior Citizens' Equity Act* to scale back this tax over the next five years to 50 percent, which is the level of benefits that were taxable prior to *OBRA 1993*.

That is not good enough. Social Security benefits were not taxed at all until 1984. Congress, in its efforts to find new revenue sources to fund its excessive spending habit, imposed a tax on beneficiaries whose income totaled $25,000 for an individual and $32,000 for couples. That law required beneficiaries to pay up to 50 percent of their benefits to the government.

The premise of these taxes is simple: penalize seniors who are productive and who choose to stay in the workplace and earn money for their retirement and for their families. It is important to note that these seniors still pay regular income taxes on that money they earn while employed. It is the Social Security benefits that the Congressional pick-pockets have targeted. Rather than create incentives for seniors to remain active and gainfully employed, the Congress has actually created disincentives.

ESTATE TAXES

In 1987, Congress passed tax laws which imposed federal estate taxes on the estate of every person who dies and leaves assets worth more than

$600,000 (excluding assets willed to a surviving spouse or to a charity). If a taxpayer is careful, a married couple can bequeath up to $1.2 million to their heirs free from taxes, often called a "unified credit." That unified credit requires the creation of a "bypass" trust which has the effect of invoking a special "exemption" for a will or living trust in force at the time of the first spouse's death.

These estate taxes hit families hard, particularly since nearly two-thirds of all Americans die without a will.

This tax is unfair to every taxpayer, but it is particularly onerous to family-owned businesses. Politicians regularly applaud small businesses as the engine driving our economy, and point to millions of jobs being created every year by individuals who are willing to take the risk to start businesses and create jobs.

What they do not say is that the government is ready and willing to steal most of the assets these entrepreneurs have spent their lives building and which they expected they would be able to pass on to the next generation. Today, more than 70 percent of family businesses do not succeed to the next generation, and 87 percent do not survive to the third generation.

For those businesses which fail shortly after the death of the founder of the business, 90 percent say the federal estate tax was the predominant reason for the failure.

What needs to be said to the Congress to stop this fraud on American business owners and taxpayers? How can they justify praising the system that generates wealth in our economy and creates jobs for working families and then undermines it when the owner dies?

The problem is a serious one, particularly when you look at surveys that reveal that only 26 percent of family business owners say they have the liquid assets to pay estate taxes if their heirs were to inherit the business today. On average, 46 workers lose their jobs every time a family-owned business closed its doors.

In 1994, Republicans swept the Congress and promised in their "Contract With America" they would increase the amount of the "unified credit" to $750,000 over a three-year period, and allow for an annual increase thereafter indexed to the inflation rate. It would be a promise they would not fulfill.

But failure to fulfill the promise comes not from lack of trying. Every year, bills are thrown into the legislative hopper to reduce or eliminate this tax, but all die in committees because no one can come up with a method to offset the loss in revenue to the government.

That, of course, begs the question as to why there should be an offset to revenues that were unjustified in the first place.

But the arcane world of Washington is not easily understood, and the reasoning utilized by the

Congress is rarely consistent enough to develop any understandable or reliable standard by which a plan might be developed that would be approved by the Congress.

The 1997 budget law offers some relief, but it also illustrates the real problem faced by seniors who may be trying to develop a strategy to pass along their assets to their families. What is law one year, is changed the next. And there is little prospect that a tax plan developed this year will work under a new scheme concocted by the Congress in a year to two.

For example, on August 1, 1997, President Clinton appeared ready to sign two separate bills passed by Congress which comprised the 1997 budget law. Some relief was offered in estate and gift tax laws that promised to save taxpayers money, but all of the changes made the almost indecipherable law even more complex. Nearly every provision has a different enactment date, some are retroactive to various dates in 1997, while others are effective on the date of signing by the President, and others are effective in future years.

Here's the problem. If you are trying to develop a strategy to effectively convey your assets to your heirs, and you rely upon those provisions which will take effect in future years, what assurance will you have that the Congress will not modify or repeal those provisions in future budget deals? The answer: None whatsoever.

The *Taxpayers Relief Act of 1997 (TRA '97)* increased the unified credit in 1998 to $625,000; in

1999 to $650,000; in 2000 and 2001 to $675,000; and in 2002 and 2003 to $700,000. There were further projected increases which increased dramatically from 2003 through 2006 which ratcheted the unified credit to a whopping $1,000,000.

These numbers allow President Clinton and the Congress to thump their chests with the claim they have dramatically increased the unified credit. But when you look at the details, the real fraud they are perpetuating is uncovered.

In the first seven years of the phased-in increase in the unified credit, the numbers are only modest increases. That is the period which these politicians are using to project a balanced budget. When the rapid acceleration in the limits occur, they are so far out that everyone knows the Congress will tinker with them when they need money to balance the budget again.

Responding again to intense pressure from The Seniors Coalition and other senior advocacy groups, *TRA '97* does include a family-owned business exclusion. This provision allows owners of a "qualified family-owned business" to take an additional exemption of up to $1.3 million from estate taxes. Sounds good, doesn't it?

But the devil, once again, is thrashing about in the details.

To qualify for this family-owned business exemption, the decedent or members of his or her family, must have owned or materially participated in the business for at least 5 of the 8 years immediately preceding death. And the exemption can be "recaptured" by the IRS if the heirs sell the business within 10 years after the date of death. There are a myriad of other technical requirements that also apply in these situations.

This exemption grants business owners more than twice the exemption of non-business owners but does not index the $1.3 million allowance for inflation.

Some members of Congress and their staffs are quick to point to other changes in the tax law that will benefit seniors. One favorite is to point out that the annual gift tax exclusion, which is under present law the first $10,000 of gifts, will be increased beginning in 1999 to account for the cost of living inflation rate.

What they don't say is that the increases will be made only in $1,000 increments. Thus, taxpayers will likely not see any benefit from this change until 2001, assuming that some future Congress won't take this benefit away when they see the resulting reduction in revenues.

Another cynical characterization of a so-called benefit for seniors from a change in the tax law is found in Section 1309 of *TRA '97*. This change provides that certain estate tax provisions will not apply to contributions of up to $7,000 to a "qualified funeral trust."

If that sounds like good policy, you have to look behind the facade and see who really benefits. This "qualified funeral trust" can only be administered by "a person engaged in the trade or business of providing funeral or burial services or property necessary to provide such services." This clause excludes any existing third-party trust arrangement common to the establishment of estate planning strategies, which most of us would have if we need to shelter our estates from the heavy hand of the tax collecting Congress.

So why would Congress structure this benefit this way?

This favorable tax treatment appears to be a special interest tax provision designed to reward a part of the funeral industry that has a long history of marketing abusive "prepaid funeral trusts" to seniors. That simply means that this group of charlatans used the money they made off their fraudulent schemes to "buy" a special tax break.

Earnings limits and estate taxes rip-off hard working Americans who find themselves victimized by a greedy, tax-happy Congress that finds its spending priorities more important than allowing retirees to enjoy the retirement years they have earned.

SOLUTIONS:

HOW SENIORS CAN STAND UP FOR THEMSELVES

Seniors should not be the victims of the frauds that the government heaps on them. The good news is that something can be done to stop these frauds and actually change the behavior of the government to prevent flawed bills and bureaucracies from hurting seniors in the future. Here we focus on things any individual can do to protect himself from government frauds.

♦ **Call your Congressman today.** You have the right to call your Congressman's local district office and register your opinion on any issue you choose. There is a trick to getting to the right staff person, so make certain that you get past the receptionist or clerical staffer who answers the phone. The receptionist is trained to screen out constituent issues calls from those that require some hands-on assistance from a constituent services specialist, so you have to approach the call by informing the receptionist that you have a problem with a particular issue, and need to talk to a constituent services specialist. Otherwise, your call about a position on a particular issue will be added to a "tally sheet." Although these sheets are eventually reviewed by legislative staffers in your Congressman's Washington office, and perhaps even the Congressman himself, they don't get you the individual attention or answers you deserve. You want to be an effective citizen lobbyist who makes more of an impact than does a mark on a tally sheet. When you call your Congressman's local office to discuss, for instance, estate taxes, inform the receptionist that you need to talk to the constituent service specialist who handles problems with estate taxes. This is a key step in making your voice heard. When you are transferred to the constituent services specialist, first ask for the name of the legislative assistant for the Congressman or Senator who handles the estate tax issue in Washington. Retrieving a specific name will allow you to use that name in follow-up calls. Ask if the office will have that individual call you at home to discuss this issue further. That way, you don't have to pay for a toll call to Washington. If that legislative assistant doesn't return your call promptly, call the local office again and tell them you are still waiting for the return call. You will get a call back, and that call offers an important opportunity.

When you speak with a legislative assistant from Washington, aim to establish a long-term relationship with that staffer. Many Washington staffers like to have an "eyes and ears" in the home district, and you can offer that service in the context of having a "friend" on the Congressman's staff that you can contact when you need to. When you have established that relationship, you have joined the ranks of the most elite citizen lobbyists in America.

♦ **Write your Congressman.** What you write to your Congressman is important, and it will be read. Personal letters mean a great deal to both your Congressman or Senator, and the staffer who is in charge of tracking their political standing at home. Congressional staffers like to say that every one letter represents 3,000 to 5,000 constituents who feel exactly the way that you do but have not taken the time to write. Because many of these offices are understaffed, you will no doubt receive a "canned" response to your letter that will provide a solid basis for telephone discussions with the legislative assistant in Washington.

When you write back to the home district

office, include a copy of their "canned" response to your letter expressing your interest in having a more complete response. Make sure to mark **"PERSONAL AND CONFIDENTIAL"** in bold letters on the front of the envelope. By doing this, you will probably have your second letter read by the Congressman or Senator's personal secretary. That starts mental alarm bells ringing in the office, and you will then get a more personal response.

When you get that letter, call the local office and tell them you have been communicating with the Washington office and you now need to speak with the Administrative Assistant to the Congressman or Senator. "Administrative Assistant" is a Washington term describing the Congressman or Senator's Chief of Staff. If you can get through, he or she will help connect you with that legislative assistant who will be the key to a long-term effective relationship. Always remember to be polite, patient, and persistent while working with Congressional staffers and establishing your impact in Washington.

If you are asked to send in a petition on an issue you agree with, by all means, send it in. Petitions deliver powerful messages on Capitol Hill, and many Congressman will show up at a "photo-op" event just to get their picture taken with the huge stacks of petitions you have helped build. Individual letters are also important because they are used by Congressional staffers to gauge public opinion of constituents.

♦ **Attend Town Hall Meetings.** Most Congressmen and Senators hold community or "Town Hall" meetings to meet with their constituents. These meetings are typically used to tout their own legislative achievements, but you can go and express an opinion and ask questions. You should do it as often as you can, and be sure to stand up and speak when you get there.

To make your voice heard even louder, invite some friends who agree with your position on the issues to go along with you. There really is strength in numbers, and if several people stand up and address the issues you are concerned about, it will set the tone for the entire meeting and your Congressman or Senator will remember the issue was an important one. Don't be surprised if you see your Congressman or Senator mention that Town Meeting discussion on your issue in a news interview or in debate in the *Congressional Record.*

These events are democracy at work, and you have the right to be heard. If your Congressman tries to change the subject, or if he or she does not answer your question, just politely interrupt them and ask them to respond to your specific question. If you try it, you'll find it works.

♦ **Call radio talk show programs.** Calling a local talk show is not nearly as intimidating as calling a national talk show like those hosted by Rush Limbaugh or G. Gordon Liddy. It can still be a little intimidating, but your views on these issues can be a catalyst for generating calls from others who agree with you. That could lead to your Congressman or Senator hearing about these issues because these elected officials all have campaign volunteers and personal friends who listen to the talk shows religiously. In a very real sense, your views over radio waves can be a pipeline to your elected officials.

Make no mistake, radio talk shows have become an important part of the American political scene. Politicians flock to invitations to participate in these talk shows, and they monitor what is being said about them and about issues. The reason for this is that talk shows are populated by political activists who are opinion leaders in their communities. These talk shows have become mainstream political barometers on how the public perceives politicians and how the public feels about issues.

Remember that talk show hosts try to keep their shows moving, and they often try to be provocative and sometimes even downright rude. Just keep your cool and get your message out as concisely as possible. You might even write down what you want to say and practice it a few times before you make the call.

♦ **Write a letter to the editor.** This sounds almost too simple, and there is the nagging doubt that it may not make much of a difference. Believe it, if you write a letter to the editor talking about an issue you care about and you mention the name of an elected official, you can bet that the official will read your letter. Make your letter brief and to the point, and make certain that you comply with the requirements of the newspaper to which you are writing. These requirements are generally printed on the same page where the letters to the editor are published.

♦ **Contribute to effective senior lobbying groups.** There are a number of senior advocacy groups in Washington which really do represent your views. When you find one, make contributions you can afford because they can deliver the message with great power. This book is published by one of the best senior advocacy groups, The Seniors Coalition, the only seniors group named by the prestigious *Roll Call* newspaper, as among the ten most effective lobbying groups on Capitol Hill. Your contribution, when combined with that of tens of thousands of others, forms the basis for the kind of high-powered lobbying campaign that you need to counter those who would oppose senior issues.

Whether you make a contribution or not, many of these groups have local citizen lobbyist programs that you can join. You will receive special briefings on issues of concerns to seniors and then be given directions on how to contact your Congressman or Senator. Often these contacts include face-to-face meetings with your Congressman or Senator or their key staff members. The Seniors Coalition calls its citizens lobbying group "SCAT," for Seniors Coalition Action Teams. If you want to join this group, you can simply make a toll free call to (800) 325-9891 and say that you want to be a SCAT member. It's that easy.

You can also motivate change by working with other seniors as a group. Sometimes it requires a little initiative on the part of one person to get the ball rolling, but often these group activities can pay big dividends.

1. **Form/Attend Senior Coffee Meetings.** Senior Coffee Meetings allow neighborhood seniors to meet together on a regular basis to discuss issues of concern to them. Every two or three meetings, invite an elected official to

attend and talk about issues important to the group. Whether it's a city councilman, a mayor, a county supervisor/commissioner or a Member of Congress, you will be pleasantly surprised at the willingness of these elected officials to accept your invitation.

You should call the office of the elected official you would like to invite and ask to speak with the scheduler. Tell the scheduler that you would like to extend an invitation for the elected official to speak to your group. Tell them how long the group has been meeting, and how many members you have. Then try to be flexible to accommodate the schedule of the elected official. Once you get one of these elected officials to attend, be sure to mention the name of that elected official to the schedulers of other elected officials you call for future appointments.

This technique works, and you can be very successful in communicating with your elected officials with a minimum of effort.

2. **Become a Senior Center Opinion Leader.** Almost every community has a senior center where fellow senior citizens participate in joint activities and programs. You can ask the director of your senior center to have issue seminars where speakers are invited to talk about important senior issues. You could volunteer to coordinate a day to visit your State Legislature when it is in session,

and you can lead a group of seniors to visit your local offices of your Congressman and Senators.

When you become such a leader, you will be able to promote an active approach to solving problems, energizing friends and other seniors who share your views but who lack the knowledge of how to get the ball rolling.

All of the frauds discussed in this book exist only because the government or some friends of the tax and spend crowd are allowed to get away with them. You can make a difference, and by joining with tens of thousands of other seniors, you can form a network that those responsible for these frauds cannot ignore. We can do what James Thurber's mother should have done — muzzle that "terribly strong" dog. We can and must muzzle those who try to defraud America's seniors for their own gain.